River Manifold Walks
Flash – Dovedale and Ilam

River Manifold Walks
Flash – Dovedale and Ilam

George Shufflebotham and Phil Rushton
Stoke/Newcastle-under-Lyme Ramblers' Group

Published by Sigma Leisure – an imprint of
Sigma Press, Stobart House, Pontyclerc, Penybanc Road
Ammanford, Carmarthenshire SA18 3HP

British Library Cataloguing in Publication Data

A CIP record for this book is available from the British Library

ISBN: 978-1-85058-912-9

Typesetting and Design by: Sigma Press, Ammanford, Carms

Maps: Bute Cartographics
Contains Ordnance Survey data © Crown copyright and database right 2011

Photographs: © George Shufflebotham. Manifold Trail Logo on waymarks designed by Colin Beats

Cover photographs: above: The River Manifold with Ilam Hall in the background; below: Thors Cave

Printed by: Berforts Group Ltd

Disclaimer: The information in this book is given in good faith and is believed to be correct at the time of publication. Care should always be taken when walking in hill country. Where appropriate, attention has been drawn to matters of safety. The author and publisher cannot take responsibility for any accidents or injury incurred whilst following these walks. Only you can judge your own fitness, competence and experience. Do not rely solely on sketch maps for navigation: we strongly recommend the use of appropriate Ordnance Survey (or equivalent) maps.

Foreword

For many years, the Ramblers Stoke/Newcastle-under-Lyme Group has worked closely with Staffordshire County Council to maintain public rights of way in the North Staffordshire area. In more recent times, the authors assisted by David Shea and Pauline Shufflebotham have devised and recorded linear walks following the course of Staffordshire rivers which include short circular walks along the length of those watercourses. This book details walks from the source of the River Manifold in the high and remote moorlands at Flash on the Derbyshire County boundary. The walks and river terminate in the beautiful and popular wooded valleys of Ilam and Dovedale where the Manifold becomes a tributary of the River Dove.

The linear trail of 23 miles, from where all the circular walks commence, is indicated by very distinctive footpath waymark signs throughout its length. It is clearly shown as the Manifold Trail on the 2010 edition of the Ordnance Survey Outdoor Leisure 24 White Peak Area map. The circular walks vary between 3 and 9 miles and, inevitably, some are more physically testing than others. However, an indication of the terrain and likely effort required is provided within the description of each walk.

The detailed descriptions of the walks are designed to give confidence to those who are unsure of following public rights of way outside the popular and very frequented areas of walking tourism. Do carry a compass. All that is needed is to identify the points of the compass which are often referred to within the description of the walks. This is necessary because there are areas where the paths may be indistinct and a little difficult to locate.

All the routes within this book, after being described and recorded, were proof-walked by volunteers to ensure that the ability to read a map was not an essential skill to complete the walks and to guarantee, as far as possible, that the outstanding beauty of the Staffordshire Moorlands and Peak District will be enjoyed. However, why not take the opportunity to follow the walks on the Ordnance Survey map of the area (Ordnance Survey Map Outdoor Leisure 24 White Peak)? It is a really good and easy way to gain the confidence to explore the more remote areas of the British countryside and it is certainly the key for escape from maddening crowds.

George Shufflebotham and Phil Rushton
September 2011

Contents

The Countryside Code

Be safe, plan ahead and follow any signs
Even when going out locally, it is best to get the latest information about where and when you can go: for example, your rights to go onto some areas of open land may be restricted while work is carried out, for safety reasons or during breeding seasons. Follow advice and local signs, and be prepared for the unexpected.

Leave gates and property as you find them
Please respect the working life of the countryside, as our actions can affect people's livelihoods, our heritage, and the safety and welfare of animals and ourselves.

Protect plants and animals, and take your litter home
We have a responsibility to protect our countryside now and for future generations, so make sure you don't harm animals, birds, plants or trees.

Keep dogs under close control
The countryside is a great place to exercise dogs, but it's every owner's duty to make sure their dog is not a danger or nuisance to farm animals, wildlife or other people.

Consider other people
Showing consideration and respect for other people makes the countryside a pleasant environment for everyone – at home, at work and at leisure.

The Manifold Trail linear walk from Flash to Dovedale

This walk is designed as a linear walk of 23 miles. It has been split into three sections, but can be completed in one day by the more ardent walker.

1st section Flash to Longnor
Approximately 8 miles
This section of the walk is very hilly and can be quite wet but, nevertheless, it is well waymarked and certainly worth the effort.

If only walking the first section, one car needs to be parked in or near the village square at Longnor (situated on the A5053 Leek/Longnor road) and the other at The Knights' Table at The Travellers Rest, at Flash (on the A53 Leek/Buxton road).

2nd section Longnor to Wetton Mill
Approximately 7½ miles
This section is quite flat.

If only walking the second section, one car needs to be parked at Wetton Mill in the Manifold Valley (reached via Butterton) and the other in or near the village square at Longnor.

3rd section Wetton Mill to Ilam
Approximately 7½ miles
This section is a little hilly but again worth the effort.

If only walking the third section, one car needs to be parked at Dovedale Stepping Stones Car Park in Ilam and the other at Wetton Mill.

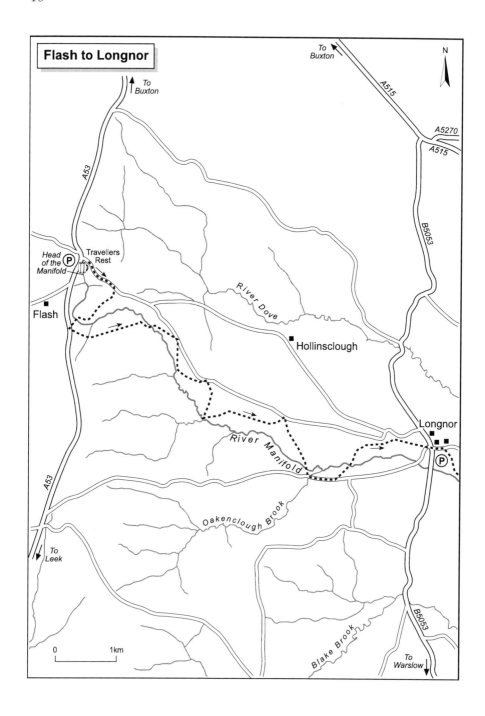

Flash to Longnor

Section 1
Flash to Longnor

Flash situated at 1518ft on the A53 Leek to Buxton road, is the highest village in the country thus making The Knights' Table (at The Travellers Rest) at Flash Bar, famous for its different ales, one of the highest situated pubs in the country. The village of Flash was famous for its counterfeit money in years gone by and also for prize fighting. The River Manifold rises at Flash Bar.

The Knight's Table

Walk directions

1. The walk commences at the Travellers Rest public house on the A53 road at Flash Head.

2. Take the road towards Longnor by the side of the public house and head towards Summer Hill Farm which can be seen about a mile in the distance.

3. Keep on the Longnor road past the farm and, after approximately 200 yards, take the stile into the field on the right (opposite Colshaw Road).

4. Cross the field in the direction as indicated by the finger post and follow waymarked signs to cross further fields by gates onto moorland (look left towards Longnor to see the impressive Parkhouse and Chrome (Dragon's Back) hills.

5. Cross the moor in a south-easterly direction towards the white painted Black Bank Farm on the hillside opposite. This is a 'right to

Dragons Back Hills

roam' area. From the top of the moor you will see Nields Farm on the valley floor, which is your next destination.

6. Follow the track to right of the farm as indicated by waymarks.

7. Follow the track into a steep gully where it crosses the infant River Manifold gushing from the hillside.

8. Continue steeply up the track to exit onto the major A53 Leek/Buxton road, but immediately turn left and left again to enter an almost parallel farm track protected by a cattle grid. The track is waymarked and the direction is now due east.

9. With Nields Farm visible on the left, follow the track to pass in front of the white painted Black Bank Farm. Exit the farm over a stile into a small paddock and, within 40 yards, leave by a stile on your left to descend into the valley in the direction of the waymark.

10. Keep to an easterly bearing and head over the moor towards a lone tree on the hilltop. A stile over the electric fence is to the left of the tree.

11. Once over the stile keep straight ahead with the stone wall on your right and Chrome Hill in front in the distance. Cross a further stile keeping straight ahead, still in an easterly (slightly north easterly) direction. Pass by a plantation of trees keeping close to the wall.

12. On leaving the plantation, turn right over a stile (as signed) and head into the valley and towards Dunn Cows Grove Farm (the direction now is still east).

13. Exit onto the farm road and cross over and through a stile in an easterly direction. Climb the gorse covered hill and note the River Manifold in the valley on the right.

Old stone clapper bridge at Dunn Cows Grove Farm

14. The path follows a wire fence and is clearly signed. On reaching a metal gate, keep left and head towards a stile on the hilltop (with the wire fence still on your right).

15. After a further stile on the hillside, the path leaves the fence to climb the hilltop. Exit onto the Flash to Longnor road and turn right, but after 30 yards turn right down the farm drive to Thickwithens Farm.

16. Exit the farmyard to pass on the right of a barn and follow waymarked signs towards the valley floor.

17. On reaching the valley floor do not cross the bridge over the River Manifold, but turn left climbing steps over a stone wall to cross marsh land, over a stile and then back up the steep valley side in a south-easterly direction.

18. Just prior to the edge of a copse of trees, turn in an easterly direction and locate a wire fence in which there is a stile.

19. Cross the open hillside in an easterly direction to the hilltop and the Flash to Longnor road. Do not exit onto the road, but bear right down a farm track towards the valley floor in a southerly direction.

20. Prior to reaching the farm building, a notice and finger post directs the path right from the track, steeply down towards the valley floor (note the superb Staffordshire Moorlands views).

21. Cross two stiles and follow waymarked signs to the valley floor. Do not cross the bridge over the growing River Manifold, but turn left by way of steps over a stone wall to take an easterly direction.

22. Cross diagonally the gently rising valley side and follow the direction signs to exit through a metal gate onto a track.

23. Turn right along the track in an easterly direction with a stone wall on the right.

24. Follow the track to Ball Bank House Farm and pass to the left of the farm buildings. This track ceases to be a public right of way by the

farm house and the path bears sharp left up the steep hillside to exit into a field by steps over a stone wall, next to a metal farm gate.

25. Follow the direction sign through two fields, the latter accessed by steps over a stone wall and exit by steps onto a tarmac road. The junction of that road with the Flash to Longnor road is only a few

Longnor
Longnor is a mediaeval village with pubs, shops, tearoom and craft centre, fish and chip shop and toilets. Some of the TV series *Peak Practice* was filmed here. We often saw some of the actors when we passed through on our walks. The Harpur Crewe Family were Lords of the Manor here. Until recent years the building directly opposite the tea rooms was a pub called the Crewe and Harpur Arms. Ye Olde Cheshire Cheese pub, a favourite with walkers, is just up the road towards Bakewell. This was a local cheese store in the 1600s and it is said that the pub is haunted by a former landlady.

St Bartholomew's Church
Founded in 1223

(more detailed information inside the church)

Situated down to the right of the churchyard, is the gravestone of William Billinge who was born, in 1679, in a cornfield at Fawfieldhead. He fought in Gibraltar in 1704, the Battle of Ramillies in 1706 and for his King in 1715 and 1745. He lived until he was 112 years old (see below).

yards on your left but turn right and head downhill towards the distant Longnor to Leek road.

26. Follow the road downhill and cross over the now substantial River Manifold, before reaching the Leek to Longnor road.

27. Turn left towards Bridge House Farm and head towards the woodland directly ahead.

28. On reaching the woodland, leave the road turning left as indicated by the finger post and head in a north-easterly direction towards Fawside Farm which can be seen directly ahead.

29. Descend into the valley and cross a small footbridge before climbing to Fawside Farm. Pass through the farmyard leaving by the driveway. However, keep close to the fence on your right because after only a few yards the driveway bears left towards the road to Flash, but the footpath remains by the fence to continue straight ahead and through a small copse of trees.

30. A stile leads into a field which you descend towards the river and a small footbridge, somewhat concealed by trees. Cross the river and then a field, which can be very wet under foot, to reach a stile in a stone wall directly ahead. At this point climb diagonally right to a stone wall and squeezer stile. Your path is now straight ahead with a further stone wall on your left.

31. A short walk brings you to the right side of a farm situated at the end of Gauledge Lane, Longnor. Enter the lane via the gates and turn right to walk the short distance to the village centre.

Refreshments

Longnor Tea Rooms and Craft Centre
Formerly the Market Hall
January to Mid February – open Saturday and Sunday Only, 10.00am to 5.00pm
Mid February to Christmas Eve – Open Every day, 10am to 5.00pm
Telephone: 01298 83587

The Horseshoe Inn
Market Place Longnor
Telephone: 01298 83262
The Horseshoe Inn the oldest surviving pub in the village dated 1609.

The Horseshoe Inn, Longnor

Section 2
Longnor to Wetton Mill

Walk Directions

1. From Longnor square, turn left in the direction of Bakewell and follow the road past the Cheshire Cheese public house to turn right within 30 yards as indicated by the finger post.

2. Walk through the farm yard keeping left to pass between the buildings and through the metal gate into a small field.

3. Cross the field diagonally to the right as indicated and over stone steps to turn right at a finger post marked 'Brund via Riverside'

4. Pass through the gap (squeezer stile) in the stone wall and head straight across the field towards a further squeezer stile. The river is now on the right and, looking left, you can see excellent examples of medieval strip farming.

Medieval strip farming

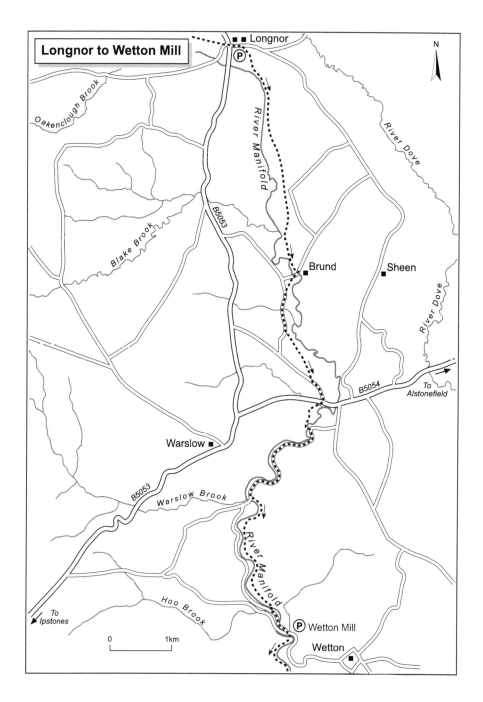

Longnor to Wetton Mill

5. Your path now follows the river valley to the hamlet of Brund, two miles distant and it is well signed throughout its route. Keeping the river on your right, you pass through several wooden gates and stiles and also cross a farm track to Over Boothlow Farm. After crossing a stile in a large hedgerow you pass close to the right of Lower Boothlow Farm through a stone squeezer stile, over a farm track and then through a metal gate.

6. Pass close to the left of a stone barn (visible from the farm) and follow waymarked signs to reach a sunken track to the right of Ridge End Farm.

Brund Mill
Originally built in 1760 as a corn mill, Thomas Cantrell converted it to a cotton mill in 1790. After getting into financial trouble it was later used for grinding corn before finally being changed to its present status as a dwelling house. Most of the machinery was retained.

7. Cross over the track which is bordered by stone walls and follow waymarks straight ahead towards Brund, crossing the stone clapper bridge over a small stream at Poole Farm.

8. Continue to follow the waymarked signs, carefully noting that the path soon bears left, as indicated by a finger post, to the side of the River Manifold.

9. Your path follows the riverside for a few yards before the river turns to the right and the path continues straight ahead towards Brund. Follow the frequent waymarked signs.

10. Exit onto the tarmac road at Brund (Mill House), follow the road to the right towards Hulme End and pass over the road bridge at Brund Mill (now apartments) – see photograph on previous page.

11. About 150 yards after the bridge, turn left off the road and into a field, as indicated by a finger post. Cross the field diagonally to the right and exit onto a tarmac road and turn left towards Hulme End.

12. About ¼ mile ahead, and just after a right bend in the road, take the stile on the left (it is waymarked but concealed by a hedge and easy to miss). Your direction is south and the path is straight ahead.

Nan Tor Cave

13. Follow waymarked signs across several fields to exit again onto the Hulme End road.

14. At this point, turn left and follow the road into the village of Hulme End at the junction with the Hartington to Warslow road. Turn right towards Warslow but, within 30 yards, turn left through a gate into the grounds of the Visitor Centre (toilets here) and onto the Manifold Valley cycle and pedestrian track.

15. Turn right and follow the valley track, the compass bearing being south west.

16. After about 250 yards, turn left off the track, over a stile. Cross the field in a southerly direction towards and over a board-walk, which assists passage across an area which can be very wet and marshy. If this area should prove too wet to traverse, change your course by returning to the Manifold cycle and pedestrian track to continue towards Wetton Mill and to the junction of that track with the Ecton to Warslow road (you must leave the track at that point to turn left and then right onto the vehicular road towards Wetton Mill).

17. If you successfully cross the marshy area, follow the Manifold Trail signs which take you over the River Manifold bridge and onto a tarmac road at Westside Mill. Turn right along that road with the River Manifold immediately on the right (note the old mine entrance on the left of the road immediately after the junction with the back of Ecton Road).

Ecton Copper Mine entrance

18. At the first road junction, which is the Ecton to Warslow road, keep left to follow the vehicular road towards Wetton Mill, which passes directly beneath Ecton Hill.

19. Just before reaching the road bridge over the River Manifold, leave the road by turning left onto a tarmac track accessed by a metal farm gate. The river continues to flow on the right.

20. Exit the track at its end at Dale Farm and turn right along the farm track towards Wetton Mill (café and toilets). Cross the bridge over the river and onto the Manifold cycle and pedestrian track.

Wetton Mill

Places of interest on route

Ecton Copper Mine
18th Century mine. One of the largest and richest in the country and owned by the Duke of Devonshire.

Nan Tor Cave
Once a flint workshop. There is a short footpath up to the cave from the premises of Wetton Mill farm and café.

Manifold Visitor Centre
Former Booking Office and Engine Shed of the Manifold Valley Light Railway
Opening times:
Sundays – February to November
Weekends – March to October
Most days during school holidays
Winter: 10.00am to 4.00pm
Summer: 10.00am to 5.00pm

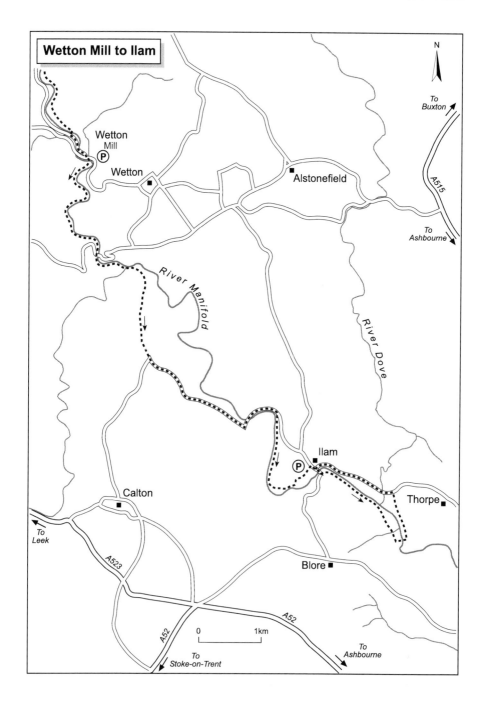

Section 3
Wetton Mill to Ilam

Walk Directions

1. Having crossed the River Manifold at Wetton Mill, turn left onto the Manifold cycle and pedestrian track and head towards Wetton and Thors Cave.

2. Continue along the track crossing over the Wetton road. Note Thors Cave high upon the left, once a home for bears and the site of Bronze Age burials.

Thors Cave – approximately 250 ft above the river.
A steep climb but worth it for the views

3. Continue on the track to cross the Grindon road at Weags Bridge. At this point, leave the cycle and pedestrian track to take the farm road which runs parallel and to the left of the track and directly alongside the river bank. You are now nearing the junction of the Rivers Manifold and Hamps.

4. At the site of a small caravan park, where the old wooden railway refreshment house still stands, cross the bridge over the River Hamps at the point where it joins the River Manifold.

5. After about 150 yards, leave the track immediately before Beeston Tor Farm to take the waymarked path on the right which climbs

Throwley Old Hall
Throwley Old Hall is open to the public. The ruins stand on the site of a former medieval landscape where ridge and furrow farming was practiced. An interesting visit with lots of information on site.

towards Throwley Old Hall and Ilam. The views open out as you ascend with the river and valley to the left. You pass to the right of an old stone barn and after about 300 yards you reach a large wooden gate blocking the track. Bear to your left as indicated by waymark signs on the gate and leave the track to climb the steep hill on its left.

6. After reaching the top of the steep hill, exit the field through a wooden gate and continue directly ahead towards Throwley Hall Farm, still out of sight but only a few hundred yards distant.

7. On nearing the farm, leave the well defined farm track and bear slightly right crossing the field and heading for a row of trees to enter the farm between the buildings, entering by the waymarked gate. Keep straight ahead through the farmyard and exit onto the tarmac road leading to Ilam. The ruins of Throwley Old Hall can be seen on the left.

8. Follow the road along the valley side and pass Rushley Farm on your right. Here the road bears sharply left to reach Rushley Bridge over the River Manifold.

9. Continue along the road towards Ilam and, as the road begins to rise, note River Cottage (1840) on the right. At that point, leave the road to take the path on your right through the garden of the cottage to reach the left of the River Manifold.

10. This footpath is a concessionary or permissive path, access by kind permission of the cottage owner and the National Trust at Ilam Hall. The path is not a public right of way and in the unlikely event of it being closed, temporarily or permanently, you will need to continue along the road to the centre of Ilam village, from where you can continue to the end of this linear walk.

11. However, having taken the concessionary footpath to the riverside, continue into the grounds of Ilam Hall with the river on your right. The footpath is known as 'Paradise Walk'. Follow the path until you reach a point where a footbridge spans the river. Here, the path divides. To your left it climbs uphill to follow a public right of way, but straight ahead it continues as a concessionary path through a

metal gate and with the river still on your right. After a short distance and on your left by the side of the path, you will see the 'Battle Stone' dated back to the 11th century and associated with the struggle between the Saxons and the Danes.

12. Ignore the paths on the left leading to the Hall, toilet, National Trust shop and car park until the stone bridge over the River Manifold comes into view. At this point the path bears left and climbs towards the Ilam Hall and village church. Follow that path to pass in front of the Hall and then turn right to pass alongside the left side of the ancient church. At this point the footpath becomes a public right of way leading to the village centre.

13. Exit onto the Stanhope to Alstonfield road at the village centre and turn right to reach the Ilam Cross, known also as the Mary Watts Memorial. At the cross, carry straight on towards Blore, crossing the stone river bridge before leaving the road by steps and a stile leading to the right side of the river.

14. Follow the river bank which is on your left in a southerly direction, over several fields until you enter a small copse of trees. At this point, the path climbs above the river and you will need to look

Ilam Hall was built in Tudor Gothic style for Mr Jesse-Watts Russell between 1821-1826

Ilam Church
The church originally dates from Saxon times, though little from this era can still be seen. It is associated with St Bertram, the hermit whose wife was killed by wolves. His tomb and two Saxon crosses can be seen in the churchyard. The tomb is a place of pilgrimage. There is an extensive leaflet available inside the church which is usually open to visitors.

very closely to your left to see the River Manifold joining the River Dove as a tributary.

15. This is the point where the Manifold Trail Linear Walk comes to an end. Unless you decide to retrace steps back to Ilam village, it is necessary to continue for a short distance to the Coldwall river bridge, to turn left and then left again in order to return to Ilam village along the footpath on the other side of the River Dove.

16. Just before the point where the two rivers meet, the path bears right to cross fields and exit onto the Ilam to Thorpe road. Turn left

along the road to continue for a little more than half a mile to reach Ilam village centre.

Note: The deviation to Coldwall Bridge can be muddy and will add about 1 mile to the total distance of this linear walk.

Coldwell Bridge over an old deserted coaching road

Refreshments

Ilam Hall
Although Illam Hall is not open to the public and is now used as a Youth Hostel, there is however a National Trust Shop and Information Centre in the old cellar of the Hall and tea rooms in the stables at the rear.

Index to Circular Walks

Key to degree of difficulty
A Easy
B Climb Involved
C Moderately Testing

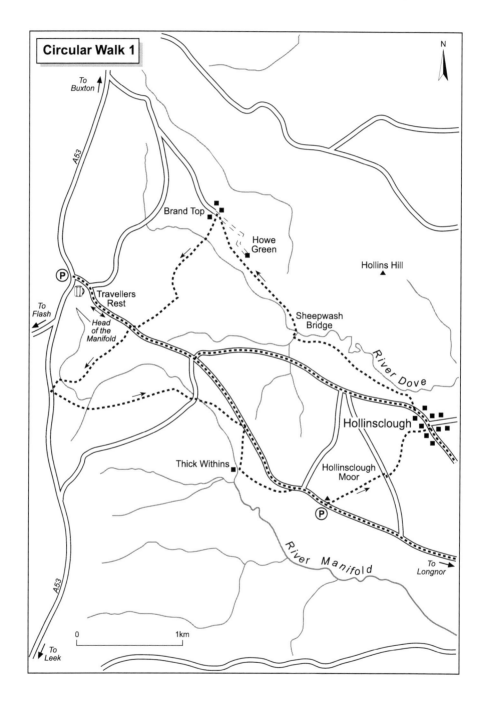

Circular Walk 1

To Buxton
A53
Brand Top
Howe Green
Hollins Hill
P
Travellers Rest
To Flash
Head of the Manifold
Sheepwash Bridge
River Dove
Hollinsclough
Thick Withins
Hollinsclough Moor
P
River Manifold
To Longnor
A53
To Leek

0   1km

N

Walk 1
Flash, Hollingsclough, Flash

A walk, which for the most part passes over remote moorland. The directions given should make it easy to follow but such is the terrain that a compass is essential and an Ordnance Survey Map advisable. The route is undulating and the paths often uneven and sometimes wet. That said, the walk provides a fine experience of the high Staffordshire Moorlands with excellent hilltop views over wild and generally unspoilt moors. A moderately testing walk for the more experienced rambler who may be seeking fresh air, exercise and a little bit of solitude.

Distance	7½ miles
Duration	5 hours
Parking	Flash Bar – free parking and at the public house, with licensee's permission
Refreshments	Travellers' Rest public house (presently named 'Knight's Table') and shop café

Walk Directions

The walk commences at the public house at Flash on the A53 road near Buxton and, for approximately 3 miles, it follows the route of the Manifold Trail Walk with its distinct waymark signs.

1. Take the road towards Longnor by the side of the public house and head towards Summerhill Farm, which can be seen about a mile in the distance.

2. Keep on the Longnor road past the farm and, after approximately 200 yards, take the stile into a field on the right (opposite Colshaw

Road). Cross the field in the direction as indicated by a finger post and follow waymark signs to cross a second field by gates onto moorland. Look left towards Longnor to see the impressive Parkhouse and Chrome (Dragons Back) Hills. According to the book *Highways and Byeways of Derbyshire* by Nelly Erichsen, Chrome Hill is reputed to be haunted from midnight to daybreak by 'The Prince of Darkness', so beware!

3. Cross the moor in a south-westerly direction towards the white painted Black Bank Farm on the hillside opposite. This is a 'Right to Roam Area'. From the top of the moor, you will see Nields Farm on the valley floor, which is your next destination.

4. Follow the track to the right of the farm as indicated by waymarks.

5. Follow the track into a steep gully where it crosses the infant River Manifold gushing from the hillside.

A lone tree on the hilltop

6. Continue steeply up the track to exit onto the major A53 Leek to Buxton road, but immediately turn left and left again to enter an almost parallel farm track protected by a cattle grid. The track is waymarked and the direction is now due east.

7. With Nields Farm visible on the left, follow the track to pass in front of Black Bank Farm. Exit the farm over a stile into a small paddock and, within 40 yards, leave by a stile on your left to descend into the valley in the direction of the waymark sign.

8. Keep to an easterly bearing and head over the moor towards a lone tree on the hilltop. There is a stile over the electric fence to the left of the tree.

9. Over the stile, keep straight ahead with a stone wall on your right and Chrome Hill in front in the distance. Cross a further stile, keeping straight ahead in a slightly north-easterly direction. Pass by a plantation of trees keeping close to the wall.

10. On leaving the plantation, turn right over a stile (as signed) and head into the valley and towards Dunn Cows Grove Farm (direction now, still east).

Clapper bridge at Dunn Cows Grove Farm

11. Exit onto a farm road and cross over and through a stile in an easterly direction. Climb the gorse covered hill and note the River Manifold in the valley on the right.

12. The path follows a wire fence and is clearly signed. On reaching a metal gate, keep left and head towards a stile on the hilltop (the wire fence is still on your right).

13. After a further stile on the hillside, the path leaves the fence to climb the hilltop. Exit onto the Flash to Longnor road and turn right

Looking back to Dunn Cows Grove Farm from a hilltop stile

and, after 30 yards, turn right down a farm drive to Thick Withens Farm.

14. Exit the farmyard to pass on the right of barn and follow waymark signs towards the valley floor.

15. On reaching the valley floor do not cross the bridge over the River Manifold, but turn left climbing steps over a stone wall to cross marshland, over a stile and then back up the steep valley side in a south-easterly direction.

16. Just prior to the edge of a copse of trees, turn left in an easterly direction and locate a wire fence in which there is a stile.

17. Cross the open hillside in an easterly direction to the hilltop and the Flash to Longnor road. Leave the Manifold Trail walk at this point to cross a stile onto the Flash to Longnor road, and then turn right to walk along the road for about 250 yards to a large lay-by

Hollingsclough

The village of Hollingsclough is on the old silk road and was famous for its silk button industry. Goods were transported down this road. The Methodist Chapel was built in 1801 by John Lomas, a jaggerman.

Approaching Hollingsclough

on the right. From the hilltop at this point the view, to your right, is over the valley of the River Manifold and, to your left, the valley of the River Dove.

18. Just 30 paces after the lay-by note the rough track on your left, which you must take to descend over the heather covered Hollingsclough Moor. Your compass bearing is north-easterly and the impressive view of the hills of High Wheeldon, Parkhouse and Chrome (Dragon's Back) is directly ahead.

19. The lane leads to a narrow tarmac road where you turn right, and then left onto a further road after only a few yards. This area is shown on the Ordnance Survey Map (White Peak Area) as 'Coatestown'. Remain on that lane to pass Coatestown Farm but, where the road bears sharply right, you need to continue straight ahead to descend a very rough track to the village of Hollingsclough. The tranquillity, which generally exits in the vicinity of these tracks, is often shattered during weekends by the passage of motor cycles; machines which are no doubt responsible for the unevenness of the ground underfoot.

20. On reaching the village of Hollingsclough turn sharp left to follow the old silk road in front of the Methodist Chapel (refreshments are available at the Church Hall on the opposite side of the road but only on Sunday mornings). Pass by the chapel to climb the road for about 200 yards, where you turn right through a wooden gate as

indicated by a fingerpost. You are now entering the area known as Hollingsclough Rake, and there is a splendid view of the unique hills of Chrome and Parkhouse in the distance on your right.

21. After only about 20 yards the path divides, one heading downhill towards the infant River Dove (due north) and the other straight ahead to proceed parallel to the river in the valley below. Continue straight ahead. The route can be muddy in places but the absence of pathside barriers ensures that this is not a great problem.

22. The path is very evident and easy to follow but, shortly before the end of the valley, you will note that it again divides, with a grassy track leading uphill to the left and a waymark path straight ahead, which passes a stone barn. You continue ahead (in a northerly direction) as the path gradually descends towards the river and valley floor.

23. A stone clapper bridge over a stream leads to a stile, which you cross to reach Washgate Bridge and the river ford, which is immediately in front of it. The stoney packhorse way passes over the bridge and ford at this point. You turn right to follow it over the bridge, then to climb the track, which bears right, then left, and then right again. On this corner, note the gate above and on the left of the track. It may be partially hidden by vegetation but a waymark sign on a fence post gives good indication of its location.

24. Pass through that gate to follow the stone wall on the left (direction north-westerly). The River Dove is now on your left at the bottom of a very deep and wooded gorge. The path gradually descends to meet the river over a stone clapper bridge. You then cross a stile to begin a steady climb up the fern covered side of the steep valley. The path veers left and right for ease of ascent but your general compass direction remains north-west.

25. A fingerpost at the top of the hill indicates two paths. Follow the path on your left and, on reaching the next stile, you may see traffic on the A53 Leek to Buxton road in the far distance. Continue on the path twisting through ferns and vegetation on the hillside, but your direction is still north-west with the valley floor and river on your left.

26. You head towards the stile very visible on the hilltop. A waymark on that stile indicates your path, which is due north and passes to the right of nearby derelict buildings. Look a few hundred yards ahead and note a derelict stone house on the hilltop. Climb the field and, just prior to that derelict building, exit the field onto a rough track. Turn left to pass in front of the property but then turn immediately, again left, to follow the footpath, which passes alongside the right of the building. You then commence a steep descent towards the valley floor and the river. Look ahead to the opposite hillside and you will see Nether Colshaw Farm and a clear path leading steeply to it, which is your next destination and route.

Washgate Bridge
An old packhorse bridge – apparently the bridge was so named because the river here was a local sheep-dipping place. The sides of the bridge were built low to prevent packhorses trapping their baskets (panniers).

27. Cross the river over a stone clapper bridge and there follows a steep climb up a gully in a south-westerly direction. The route leads to a stile on the hilltop immediately before the premises of Nether Colshaw Farm. Cross that stile and continue straight ahead to enter the premises via a set of ladder steps. Pass between the left of the farmhouse and the adjoining horse paddock from where you climb further steps from the back of the house and into a field. A south-westerly direction, as indicated by waymark signs, leads over a further stile to Kings Farm. Chrome Hill can be seen behind and to your left and Axe Edge and the A53 Leek to Buxton road is on the horizon to your right.

28. Ignore the fingerpost indicating a path on your right, as you enter Kings Farm premises, and continue straight ahead to the left of the dwelling to take the farm track, which leads to a narrow tarmac lane.

29. Turn right along the lane and you will reach the junction with the Flash to Longnor road. At this point, you have rejoined the Manifold Trail (note the waymark sign opposite). Turn right here to follow the Flash to Longnor road for just over one mile to the Knights Table (Travellers' Rest) public house at Flash and the adjoining shop where coffee and refreshments provide a welcome finale to a fine bracing country walk.

Walk 2
Longnor, Hollingsclough, Longnor

A relatively long but easy walk from one of the most interesting Staffordshire Moorland villages. The scenery is impressive, the hills of Parkhouse and Chrome providing a stunning and unique background. The hamlet of Hollingsclough provides the opportunity of a welcome pause before a long but pleasant climb to the narrow ridge overlooking both the Dove and Manifold Valleys. Impressive views throughout.

Distance	7 miles
Duration	4 hours
Parking	Longnor Square – free parking
Refreshments	Longnor Tea Rooms and Craft Centre, the Village Store and public houses and the Fish and Chip Shop Café

Walk Directions

1. This walk commences from the Tea Rooms and Craft Centre in Longnor village centre. Leave the cobbled parking area in front of the tea rooms by entering Chapel Street, which is to the left of the building as you face it and next to the public toilets. Chapel Street is a cobbled entry with ancient buildings on either side, leading into Church Street by the entrance to the village church. Turn left to cross over Church Street and, immediately before the junction with the Buxton road, turn right onto a narrow tarmac lane which bears a 'no through road' sign.

2. After about 150 yards the lane bears to the left towards houses but, on your right, you will see a footpath fingerpost and a set of steps leading to a tree-lined path. Climb the steps and follow the

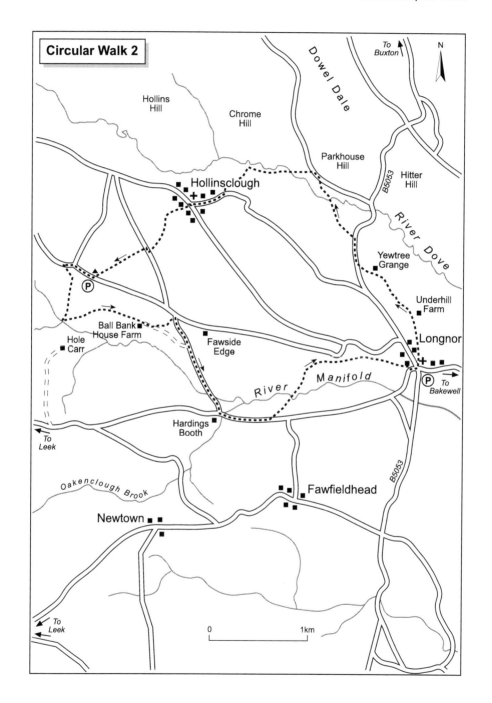

path uphill. Thirty or forty paces from the road, and at the top of the hill, the path deviates left between two trees and then immediately right to pass through the rear garden of a bungalow and then over a stile and into a field.

3. Your path is straight ahead with a stone wall on your right. Your compass bearing is due north. At the top of the field, cross a stile in a stone wall to descend towards the valley of the River Dove. Your compass bearing is still due north and, as you turn left and start to descend, the view ahead is of Hitter Hill and the jagged peaks of Parkhouse Hill. Immediately to your right is the imposing hill of High Wheeldon.

4. The path exits onto a track from Underhill Farm, along which you continue to reach a cottage at a junction of paths. Turn right at this point to follow the waymark track towards the valley floor.

5. However, on reaching a point only about 100 yards to the rear of that cottage. Note the direction sign on the second electricity pole

View of Hitter Hill & Parkhouse Hill

and leave the track here to descend right towards a thick hedge of trees and bushes. A stile is hidden in that hedge immediately before a stone cottage. Pass to the left of the cottage and note that your footpath is within a fenced area to the left of the cottage driveway.

6. The cottage driveway exits onto a tarmac lane, which passes to the left of Yew Tree Grange Farm to reach the Longnor to Buxton road. Turn right down the main road for about 300 yards and, just before the road bears sharply right towards Glutton Bridge, turn left to take a limestone track, which is protected by a metal farm gate and wooden stile. The waymark sign on the gatepost indicates the compass bearing of north-west.

7. At the end of the track follow the indication of the footpath fingerpost to enter fields, which descend to a footbridge over the River Dove. Your compass bearing to the bridge is due north and

Footbridge over the River Dove with Parkhouse Hill in the background

immediately ahead you have the close and impressive sight of Parkhouse and Chrome (Dragon's Back) Hills.

8. Exit the field onto the tarmac lane from Glutton Bridge. You are now at the base of Parkhouse Hill on which there is now the legal right to roam, provided of course one has strong legs and powerful lungs. Turn left along the tarmac lane but, after only 20 yards, bear left along the limestone track and through the impressive gateposts of Stannery Farm.

9. Continue straight ahead in a westerly direction. Chrome Hill (Dragon's Back) is on your right. There is no right to roam over Chrome Hill but there is a superb permissive path over its peak, which should be approached with care when high winds prevail. No time for Chrome Hill today, but mark it down as a must do walk for tomorrow.

10. On reaching a point near to the base of Chrome Hill, the track bears sharply left towards the village of Hollingsclough. There is a signpost at this junction of paths and your compass bearing is now south west.

11. The track exits onto the Longnor road where you turn right to enter Hollingsclough village. At the village centre you will see the chapel on your right, the Chapel Hall immediately ahead and a red telephone box to your left. Take a coffee break here if you so wish but afterwards turn neither right nor left but continue straight ahead to enter a rough track known locally as Swan Rake. Your compass bearing is south-west.

12. The track is uneven underfoot due to the passage of ancient water and present day off-road motor cycles. After about 150 yards, the track divides. Do not take the path to your left but continue steeply uphill until you reach a tarmac lane along which you continue straight ahead, still in a south westerly direction.

13. On reaching the T-junction at the top of the lane, turn right and, after only 20 yards, turn left and onto a rough track, which proceeds uphill between stone walls. This track leads over an area known as Hollingsclough Moor. There is a need to watch where you

Outstanding view of the Staffordshire Moorlands from Hollingsclough Moor

put your feet, but take time to look behind for a final view of the hills forming the valley of the River Dove.

14. The track exits onto the Longnor/Flash/Buxton road at the highest point between the valley of the River Dove and the valley of the River Manifold, into which you will shortly descend. (Note the trig point in the field on your right at the top of the track.)

15. Turn right onto the main road and walk in a north-westerly direction towards Flash. After approximately 150 yards there is a road junction to your right, but remain on the major road as it bears to the left and then, after a further 100 yards, bears to the right. At the commencement of that right bend (at the bottom of the hill), note the metal gate and wooden stile on your left, which leads to Heathylee Farm. Cross that stile and follow the track as it proceeds left towards the farm. You are now on the route of the Manifold Trail Walk with its distinctive waymark signs.

16. Prior to reaching the farm building, a notice and finger post directs the path right from the track, steeply down towards valley floor. Note the superb Staffordshire Moorlands views.

17. Cross two stiles and follow waymark signs to the valley floor. Do not cross this bridge over the growing River Manifold, but turn left by way of steps over a stone wall to take an easterly direction.

18. Cross diagonally the gently rising valley side and follow direction signs to exit through a metal gate onto track.

19. Turn right along the track in an easterly direction with a stone wall on the right.

20. Follow the track to Ball Bank House Farm and pass to the left of farm buildings. The track ceases to be a public right of way by the farmhouse. Your path bears sharp left up the steep hillside to exit into a field by steps over a stone wall, next to a metal farm gate.

21. Follow the direction sign through two fields, the latter accessed by steps over a stone wall and exit by steps onto a tarmac road. The junction of that road with the Flash to Longnor road is only a few yards on your left but turn right and head downhill towards the distant Longnor to Leek road.

22. Follow the road downhill and cross over the now substantial River Manifold, before reaching the Leek to Longnor road.

23. Turn left towards Bridge House Farm and head along the main road towards the woodland, directly ahead.

24. On reaching the woodland leave the road, turning left as indicated by the finger post, and head in a north-easterly

The substantial River Manifold

direction towards Fawside Farm, which can be seen directly ahead.

25. Descend into the valley and cross a small footbridge before climbing to Fawside Farm. Pass through the farmyard leaving by the driveway. However, keep close to the fence on your right because, after only a few yards, the driveway bears left towards the road to Flash but the footpath remains by the fence continuing straight ahead and through a small copse of trees.

26. A stile leads into a field, which you descend towards the river, and a small footbridge somewhat concealed by trees. Cross the river and then a field, which can be very wet underfoot, to reach a stile in a stone wall directly ahead. At this point climb diagonally right to a stone wall and squeezer stile. Your path is now straight ahead with a further stone wall on your left.

27. A short walk brings you to the right side of the farm at the end of Gauledge Lane, Longnor. Enter the lane via the gates and turn right to walk the short distance to the village centre.

Walk 3
Longnor, Brund, Hulme End, Longnor

An interesting walk through typical Staffordshire Moorland countryside and villages. A long but easy walk following the River Manifold to Hulme End and its tourist Visitor Centre. Superb scenery and views along the way.

Distance	9 miles
Duration	5 hours
Parking	On Longnor Village Square — free parking
Refreshments	Longnor Tea Rooms and Craft Centre, the Village Store, public houses and the Fish and Chip Shop Café. Manifold Visitor Centre, Hulme End village stores and the Manifold Inn

Walk Directions

1. This walk commences from the cobblestone square at Longnor village centre. Facilities here include public toilets, public houses, fish and chip shop, village store and craft centre with tea rooms.

2. From Longnor to Hulme End you will take the Manifold Trail Walk, with its distinctive waymark signs, to follow the River Manifold as it heads towards Dovedale.

3. From Longnor square head in the direction of Bakewell and follow the road past the Cheshire Cheese public house, to turn right within 30 yards as indicated by a finger post.

4. Walk through the farmyard, keeping left to pass between buildings and through metal gates into a small field.

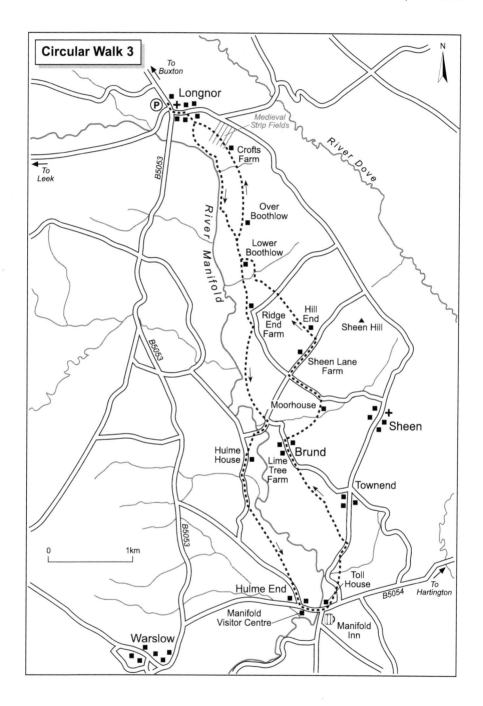

This area is known as 'Folds End'

5. Cross the small field diagonally to the right, as indicated by the sign, and then over stone steps to turn right as indicated by a finger post marked 'Brund via Riverside'.

6. Pass through a gap (squeezer stile) in the stone wall and walk across the field towards a further squeezer stile. The river is now on the right and looking left you will see excellent examples of medieval strip farming.

7. Your path now follows the river valley to the hamlet of Brund, two miles distant, and it is well signed throughout its route. Keeping the river on your right, you pass through several wooden gates and stiles and also cross a farm track to Over Boothlow Farm. After crossing a stile in a large hedgerow you pass close to the right of Lower Boothlow Farm through a stone squeezer stile, over a farm track and then through a metal gate.

8. Pass close to the left of a stone barn (visible from farm) and follow waymark signs to reach a sunken track to the right of Ridge End Farm.

9. Cross over the track, which is bordered by stone walls, and follow waymarks straight ahead towards Brund, crossing the stone clapper bridge over a small stream at Poole Farm.

10. Continue to follow waymark signs, carefully noting that the path soon bears left, as indicated by a finger post, to the side of the River Manifold. Your path follows the riverside for a few yards before the river turns to the right and the path continues straight ahead towards Brund. Follow the frequent waymark signs.

11. Exit onto a tarmac road at Brund (Mill House). Follow this road to the right towards Hulme End and pass over a road bridge at Brund Mill (now apartments).

12. About 150 yards after the bridge, turn left off the road and into a field as indicated by a finger post. Cross the field diagonally to the right and exit onto a tarmac road and turn left towards Hulme End.

13. About ¼ mile ahead, and just after a right bend in the road, take the stile on the left (it is waymarked but concealed by a hedge and easy to miss). The direction is south-east and the path is straight ahead.

14. Follow waymark signs across several fields to exit again onto the Hulme End road.

15. At this point turn left and follow the road into the village of Hulme End at the junction with the Hartington to Warslow road. To your right is the Manifold Visitor Centre with its impressive facilities of information centre, picnic area, toilets and excellent café. A visit

Hulme End Village Stores and Café

Views of Ecton Hill behind the fingerpost

is recommended. Note that the route of this walk is to the left, in the direction of Hartington, and that alternative refreshments are available at the Hulme End village stores only a few yards distant.

16. Turn left to walk along the road passing on your right an imposing old building, which houses the Riverside Bed and Breakfast facility. The adjacent Hulme End Village Stores provides refreshments and a variety of provisions.

17. Cross the road bridge over the River Manifold, passing the Manifold Inn public house on the right and the Bank House Park Campsite on the left. The road begins to climb and, at a point about 20 yards above the reception building of the campsite, you leave the road through a gap in the stone wall on your left to follow the footpath, which is indicated by a fingerpost sign. Your compass direction is north-east.

18. At the top of the field cross onto the Sheen road and turn left. Walk for only about 100 yards before leaving the road through the wall on your right. Note the fingerpost sign and your northerly compass bearing.

19. Cross a wooden stile at the next hedgerow. The path bears slightly left and downhill to cross a small stream under trees and then bears slightly right to resume a northerly route uphill. Cross a wall through stone squeezer stile and walk to a fingerpost sign on the Sheen road by a metal gateway. Turn right along the road towards Sheen but, after about 100 yards, turn left onto the driveway of Low End Farm. A fingerpost sign indicates the compass bearing of north-west (see photograph on previous page).

20. Look to your left for a panoramic view of the surrounding moorlands and Ecton Hill, the ancient site of large-scale mining. Follow the track through the farmyard but, on reaching its highest point after only a short distance, note that your route leaves the track to descend left first to a pole bearing an electricity line and then on to a metal gate in front of a copse of trees.

21. Pass through the metal gate and the wooded copse to follow the line of the stone wall on your right until you exit onto the Brund to Sheen road. Bear left along the tarmac road until you pass the New House Farm Bed and Breakfast premises on your left. At that point you will see a footpath fingerpost and a metal gate on your right. Leave the road here to climb the field diagonally to its top left corner and to a metal farm gate. Pass through the gate and follow the line of the wall on your left (compass direction is north-east).

22. Pass over a stone wall and then two further small fields before descending to cross a wire fence and , at the bottom of the hill, ford a small brook. Follow the waymark signs over a

New House Farm Bed and Breakfast

stone wall and head uphill towards an electricity pole and the top left corner of the field, where lies Moorside Farm. Turn right over the stile to follow the line of the stone wall on your right, which leads to a fingerpost sign on the far side of the farm building. Cross the wall to join the farm driveway and walk onto the Sheen road.

23. Turn left along that road and note Sheen Hill, with its cone shaped top, on your right. The trees on the hilltop in the distance on your left are at Revidge in the Reaps Moor area, 400 metres above sea level. Ecton Hill, no longer scarred by mines, is behind and to your left.

24. Continue along the road to the cross-roads and turn right in the direction of Knowl and Longnor. Pass by Sheen Lane Farm and Mushroom Cottage and then turn left into the next farm driveway which leads to Hill End Farm.

25. Before reaching the farmhouse you are requested to leave the definitive right of way through the farmyard, to take the courtesy stile on your left. That path takes you to the right over the fields in front of the farmhouse in a north-westerly direction. Walk to the top right corner of the field to cross a stone wall. Follow the line of the wall on your right and you will eventually descend into a deep tree-lined gorge at the bottom of which is a footbridge over a small stream.

26. Climb from the gorge to continue straight ahead, still in a north-westerly direction to reach the bottom corner of a stone wall. Keep the wall on your right until the path exits onto the Brund to Longnor road. Turn right here to climb the road for about 20 yards, when you will turn left onto a limestone track leading to Lower Boothlow Farm.

27. Straight ahead in the distance you will see the village of Longnor, and behind the imposing Parkhouse Hill with its unique jagged slopes.

28. Pass by the right of the farm buildings keeping close to the barn on your left. Cross the wall by a large mature tree and walk straight ahead and down the field to a stile in a stone wall. A finger post

indicates your route sharp right to cross a field to a wooden stile. At that point a path continues straight ahead to follow alongside the River Manifold towards Longnor, but your path bears right towards Over Boothlow, Farm which you can see a short distance ahead. Pass to the right of the house and continue along the track straight ahead, passing a fingerpost sign on your right, with the last of the farm buildings on your left. You will see a metal farm gate at the end of the track, but just before that metal gate there is a wooden gate in the fence on your right. Pass through that gate to cross uphill to a further fingerpost sign and a gap in a stone wall. From there continue straight ahead across the field and towards its top left corner, where you will see a stone barn.

29. Cross over the wall near to the barn and note the waymark signs indicating your path alongside the stone wall and hedge on your right. Look to your left and you will see that you are walking parallel to the River Manifold.

30. After a short distance you will reach a small derelict stone barn at a junction of paths. Ignore the path leading to the farmhouse on your right and continue past the left of the barn to reach a metal farm gate, which you will see straight ahead.

31. Pass through the gate and follow the line of the wall on your left (this area can be very muddy). At the end of the wall you cross it through a stone squeezer stile to continue ahead towards Longnor (note the River Manifold still parallel to your route and on your left). Your compass bearing is north east.

32. Follow the line of the hedge on your right and you will reach a gate at the front of Crofts Farm. Pass by and to the left of the farm to exit as indicated by a fingerpost sign onto the medieval narrow strip fields, which you cross in a north-westerly direction towards your destination of Longnor.

33. The path ends at Folds End Farm, where it joins the Manifold Trail Walk to exit through the farmyard and into the Longnor village centre.

Walk 4
Longnor, Brund, Longnor

A shorter version of Walk 3, this walk misses out the visit to Hulme End in order to commence the return ramble to Longnor at the hamlet of Brund. A lovely stroll through agricultural land bordering the River Manifold. Beautiful scenery and superb views.

Distance	5 miles
Duration	3 hours
Parking	On Longnor Square — free parking
Refreshments	Longnor Tea Rooms and Craft Centre, the Village Store, public houses and the Fish and Chip Shop Café

Walk Directions

This walk commences from the Market Square in the centre of Longnor Village. The Tea Rooms and Craft Centre are on the square as are the public toilets. The village store providing provisions and refreshments is to the left and the fish and chip shop café is to the right.

From Longnor to the village of Brund you will follow the distinctive waymark signs of the Manifold Trail Walk as it follows the path of the River Manifold to the ancient building of Brund Mill.

1. From Longnor square, walk in the direction of Bakewell and follow the road past the Cheshire Cheese public house to turn right within 30 yards, as indicated by a finger post.

2. Walk through a farmyard keeping left to pass between buildings and through metal gates into a small field.

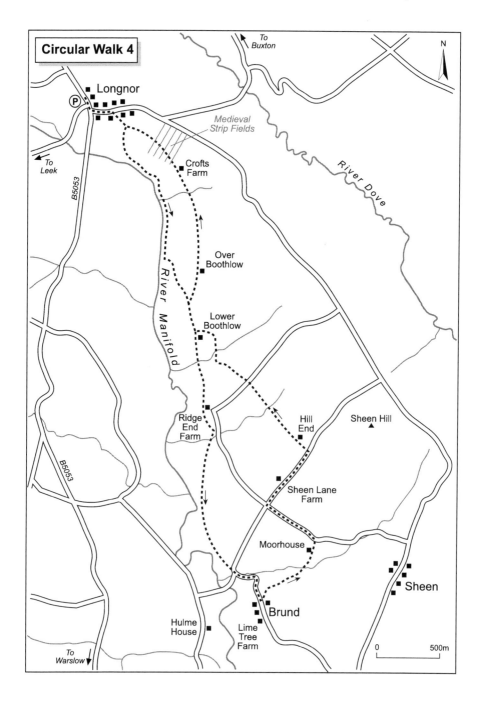

Circular Walk 4

Ye Olde Cheshire Cheese Inn
The present landlady relates that this pub is haunted by a previous landlady Thirza Robinson, who kept it between 1909-1947. Apparently her presence has often been felt by the staff at the premises. There was also a cheese factory across the road. More information can be found inside the pub.

3. Cross the small field diagonally to the right as indicated by the sign and then over stone steps to turn right, as indicated by the finger post marked 'Brund via Riverside'.

4. Pass through a gap (squeezer stile) in the stone wall and walk across the field towards a further squeezer stile. The river is now on the right and looking left you will see excellent examples of medieval strip farming.

5. Your path now follows the river valley to the hamlet of Brund, two miles distant and it is well signed throughout its route. Keeping

the river on your right, you pass through several wooden gates and stiles and also cross a farm track to Over Boothlow Farm. After crossing a stile in a large hedgerow, you pass close to the right of Lower Boothlow Farm through a stone squeezer stile, over a farm track and then through a metal gate.

6. Pass close to the left of a stone barn (visible from farm) and follow waymark signs to reach a sunken track to the right of Ridge End Farm.

7. Cross over the track, which is bordered by stone walls, and follow waymarks straight ahead towards Brund, crossing the stone clapper bridge over a small stream at Poole Farm.

8. Continue to follow waymark signs, carefully noting that the path soon bears left, as indicated by a finger post, to the side of the River Manifold. The path follows the riverside for a few yards before the river turns to the right and the path continues straight ahead towards Brund. Follow the frequent waymark signs.

9. Exit the field onto the tarmac road at Brund by the side of Mill House and turn right onto the T-junction with its direction post. Continue straight ahead on the upper road towards Sheen. The road twists left, right and left again to reach the New House Farm Bed and Breakfast premises, just before which you will see a metal gate and footpath fingerpost on your left. Leave the road here to climb the field diagonally to its top left corner to reach a metal farm gate. Pass through the gate and follow the line of the wall on your left (compass direction north-east).

10. Pass over a stone wall and then two further small fields before descending to cross a wire fence and then, at the bottom of the hill, to ford a small brook. Follow the waymark signs over a stone wall and head uphill towards an electricity pole and the top left corner of the field, where lies Moorside Farm. Turn right over the stile to follow the line of the stone wall on your right, which leads to a fingerpost sign on the far side of the farm building. Cross the wall to join the farm driveway and walk onto the Sheen road.

11. Turn left along that road and note Sheen Hill, with its cone shaped top, on your right. The trees on the hilltop in the distance on your left

View across to the cone of Sheen Hill

are at Revidge in the Reaps Moor area, 400 metres above sea level. Ecton Hill, no longer scarred by mines, is behind and to your left.

12. Continue along the road to the cross-roads and turn right in the direction of Knowl and Longnor. Pass by Sheen Lane Farm and Mushroom Cottage and then turn left into the next farm driveway, which leads to Hill End Farm.

13. Before reaching the farmhouse you are requested to leave the definitive right of way through the farmyard, to take the courtesy stile on your left. That path takes you to the right over the fields in front of the farmhouse in a north westerly direction. Walk to the top right corner of the field to cross a stone wall. Follow the line of the wall on your right and you will eventually descend into a deep tree-lined gorge at the bottom of which is a footbridge over a small stream.

14. Climb from the gorge to continue straight ahead, still in a north westerly direction, to reach the bottom corner of a stone wall. Keep

the wall on your right until the path exits onto the Brund to Longnor road. Turn right here to climb the road for about 20 yards, when you will turn left onto a limestone track leading to Lower Boothlow Farm.

15. Straight ahead in the distance you will see the village of Longnor and behind the imposing Parkhouse Hill with its unique jagged slopes.

16. Pass by the right of the farm buildings keeping close to the barn on your left. Cross the wall by a large mature tree and walk straight ahead and down the field to a stile in a stone wall. A finger post indicates your route sharp right to cross a field to a wooden stile. At that point a path continues straight ahead to follow alongside the River Manifold towards Longnor, but your path bears right towards Over Boothlow Farm which you can see a short distance ahead.

17. Pass to the right of the house and continue along the track straight ahead passing a fingerpost sign on your right and with the last of the farm buildings on your left. You will see a metal farm gate at

Folds Farm

the end of the track but just before that metal gate there is a wooden gate in the fence on your right. Pass through that gate to cross uphill to a further fingerpost sign and a gap in a stone wall. From there continue straight ahead across the field and towards its top left corner where you will see a stone barn.

18. Cross over the wall near to the barn and note the waymark signs which indicate your path alongside the stone wall and hedge on your right. Look to your left and you will see that you are walking parallel to the River Manifold.

19. After a short distance you will reach a small derelict stone barn at a junction of paths. Ignore the path leading to the farmhouse on your right and continue past the left of the barn to reach a metal farm gate, which you will see straight ahead.

20. Pass through the gate and follow the line of the wall on your left (this area can be very muddy). At the end of the wall, you cross it through a stone squeezer stile to continue ahead towards Longnor (note the River Manifold still parallel to your route and on your left). Your compass bearing is north east.

21. Follow the line of the hedge on your right and you will reach a gate at the front of Crofts Farm. Pass by and to the left of the farm to exit as indicated by a fingerpost sign onto the medieval narrow strip fields, which you cross in a north westerly direction towards your destination of Longnor. The path ends at Folds End Farm where it joins the Manifold Trail Walk to exit through the farmyard and into the Longnor village centre.

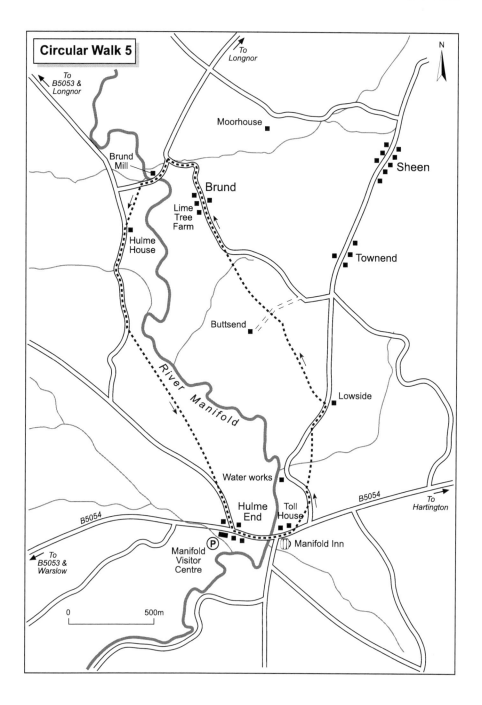

Walk 5
Hulme End, Brund, Hulme End

A short and pleasant stroll through delightful countryside. A relaxing and easy walk for all the family.

Distance	2 miles
Duration	2½ hours
Parking	Manifold Visitor Centre – pay & display car park
Refreshments	Manifold Visitor Centre, Hulme End Village Stores and The Manifold Inn

Walk Directions

This walk starts at the Manifold Visitor Centre complex at Hulme End.

The facilities at this old Manifold Valley Railway Station are excellent. There is a large car park, picnic area, toilets, shop and information centre and on the site of the old engine shed, a splendid café offering drinks and light snacks.

1. From the Visitor Centre, turn right to follow the main road in the direction of Hartington. Within a very short distance you pass the imposing old house, now the Riverside Bed and Breakfast premises and the adjacent Hulme End Village Store which caters for locals,

Riverside Bed and Breakfast

visitors, campers and walkers with general provisions and refreshments.

2. Cross the road bridge over the River Manifold passing the Manifold Inn public house on the right and the Bank House Park Campsite on ,the left. The road begins to climb and at a point about 20 yards above the reception building of the campsite, you leave the road through a gap in the stone wall on your left to follow the footpath, which is indicated by a fingerpost sign. Your compass direction is north-east.

3. At the top of the field cross onto the Sheen road and turn left. Walk for only about 100 yards before leaving the road through the wall on your right. Note the fingerpost sign and your northerly compass bearing.

4. Cross a wooden stile at the next hedgerow. The path bears slightly left and downhill to cross a small stream under trees and to bear slightly right to resume your northerly route uphill. Cross a wall

Looking back to Hulme End and Reapsmoor

*Looking left for panoramic views of the Staffordshire Moorlands
and Ecton Hill*

through a stone squeezer stile and walk to a fingerpost sign, which
is on the Sheen road by a metal gateway. Turn right along the road
towards Sheen, but after about 100 yards turn left onto the
driveway of Low End Farm. A fingerpost sign indicates the compass
bearing of north-west.

5. Look to your left for a panoramic view of the surrounding
   moorlands and Ecton Hill, the ancient site of large scale mining.
   Follow the track through the farmyard but on reaching its highest
   point after only a short distance, note that your route leaves the
   track to descend left, first to a pole bearing an electricity line and
   then on to a metal gate in front of a copse of trees.

6. Pass through the metal gate and the wooded copse to follow the
   line of the stone wall on your right until you exit onto the Brund to
   Sheen road. Bear left along the tarmac road and pass the New
   House Farm Bed and Breakfast premises on your left. After another
   50 yards or so leave the road over a stile on your left. At this point,
   there is an electricity pole and a direction fingerpost. Follow the

path indicated in a north-westerly direction to the bottom of the field, where you exit onto a tarmac road. A sign on the stile indicates that you have joined the Manifold Trail Walk. Turn left here to follow the road to Brund Mill on your right and to cross the road bridge over the River Manifold.

7. From here you follow the very distinctive Manifold Trail waymark signs for the remainder of your walk to the Hulme End Visitor Centre.

8. About 150 yards after the bridge, turn left off the road and into a field as indicated by the finger post. Cross the field diagonally to the right and exit onto a tarmac road and turn left towards Hulme End.

9. About ¼ mile ahead, and just after a right bend in the road, take stile on the left. (It is waymarked but concealed by a hedge and easy to miss). Your direction is south and the path straight ahead.

10. Follow waymark signs across several fields to exit again onto the Hulme End road.

11. At this point turn left and follow road into Hulme End. Turn right towards Warslow but, within 30 yards, turn left through gate into the grounds of the Visitor Centre.

Walk 6
Hulme End, Wetton Mill, Ecton Hill, Hulme End

This walk provides some of the most spectacular views in the Staffordshire Moorlands. It is an easy walk demanding only moderate effort, even though the steep Ecton Hill is involved. The summit of that hill is never reached. Instead the route traverses its shoulders revealing views even more splendid than those available from the very top. The areas considerable industrial past is revealed and evident but its recovery and transformation into scenic beauty is nothing short of a wonder.

Distance	6 miles
Duration	3½ hours
Parking	Manifold Visitor Centre at Hulme End
Refreshments	Wetton Mill, Manifold Visitor Centre Café, Hulme End Village Shop and The Manifold Inn

Walk Directions:

Commence the walk from the Manifold Visitor Centre at Hulme End. There is a charge for car parking but the fee is supportive of the considerable expense in maintaining the beautiful Manifold Valley area.

1. Take the Manifold Track in its south westerly direction towards Wetton Mill and Waterhouses. Note the distinctive Manifold Trail waymark signs. You will follow these until you reach Wetton Mill.

2. After about 250 yards turn left off the track and over a stile. Cross the field in a southerly direction towards, and over, a boardwalk

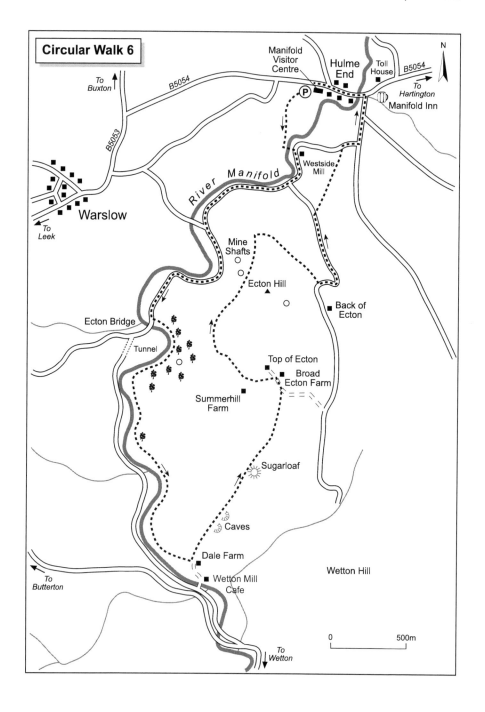

which assists passage across an area which can be very wet and marshy. If this area should prove too wet to traverse, change your course by returning to the Manifold Track to continue towards Wetton Mill and to the first junction of that track, with the road which is described at paragraph 4 below (remember to leave the track at that point to turn left and then right onto the vehicle road towards Wetton Mill).

3. If you successfully cross the marshy area follow the Manifold Trail signs which take you over the River Manifold Bridge and onto the tarmac road at Westside Mill. Turn right along that road with the river on your right (note the old mine entrance on the left of the road immediately after the junction with the Back of Ecton road).

Apes Tor Mine is one of the many mines in this area

4. Continue with the river on your right until you reach the point where your road meets the Manifold Track (mentioned at paragraph 2 above) which is now only a few yards to your right and between you and the river. At this point **do not** take the Manifold track towards Wetton Mill but keep to your left to follow the tarmac vehicular road, which passes beneath Ecton Hill. (Look for the manifold trail waymark signs!).

5. Carefully note this area as you pass. It was once highly industrialized and the platforms and loading areas, first for copper and later for cheese, are still evident by the roadsides. The cottage which was once the Mine Manager's House is on your left side of the road. More will be revealed later when you pass along the higher reaches of Ecton Hill.

6. Just before your road reaches its bridge over the River Manifold, leave the road by turning left onto a tarmac track accessed by a

metal farm gate. This enables you to continue to follow the line of the river, which is still on your right.

7. The track ends at Dale Farm. If you walk a very short distance to your right you can partake of refreshments at the Wetton Mill Café and shop where toilet facilities are also provided. However, your route for this walk requires you to turn left at Dale Farm, leaving the Manifold Trail walk to pass to the left of the farmhouse in a compass direction which is north easterly.

8. A stile at the rear of the farmhouse takes you into a steep sided valley, along which you continue. On reaching the head of that valley you will see the very prominent and rocky hill known as 'Sugar Loaf'. Your path goes up and around the left of that hill.

9. On reaching the hilltop (but not the top of Sugar Loaf), cross the stile in the wire fence and turn sharply right to pass through a stone squeezer stile some 30 yards distant. Sugar Loaf is now behind you and hidden by trees.

Sugar Loaf Hill

10. Follow the direction arrows and fingerpost to continue straight ahead (compass direction north-east). Pass through a gate as you climb the gradual gradient to leave the fields through a gate and onto a tarmac road at the area known as 'Top of Ecton'.

11. Turn left along the road to reach Broad Ecton Farm some 200 yards distant. There, two finger posts indicate your route to the left and uphill towards a row of trees on the hilltop (note the signs warning of dangerous hidden mine shafts on Ecton hillside).

12. Keep the stone wall close to your left and follow its line to the top of the field. Here it is necessary to pass through a farm gate on your left but only to reach the other side of the stone wall which you are following uphill. Continue uphill with the stone wall now on your right (compass bearing is westerly).

13. On reaching the top of that field you pass through an opening (sometimes gated) by the row of trees mentioned in paragraph 11 above. Here, your path bears slightly right (compass bearing north-west) and heads towards the very prominent corner of a stone boundary wall, some 200 yards ahead. At that point there appears to be a path continuing to the top of Ecton Hill but your route lies to your left in a westerly direction. Bear left and after only a short distance you will reach a gap in a stone wall, from where you have superb views over the village of Warslow and towards the moorlands of Blakemere. Can you spot the Mermaid Inn on the horizon?

14. Follow the waymark route downhill but only for about twenty paces before the path bears sharply right to commence its traverse around the shoulders of Ecton Hill (note the impressive Swainsley Hall in the Manifold Valley below). The spire of Grindon Church is behind and to your left (southerly direction). From here the path is narrow and usually in good order but it can be muddy and uneven if recently used by cattle.

15. Continue around the hill (compass direction north). Do not be tempted to take paths heading downhill until you pass by the depression of an old mine shaft on your right. There you reach a point where the path bears sharply to the right revealing a steep

View of Swainsley Hall and the Manifold Valley floor from Ecton Hill

drop to the valley floor immediately ahead of you with a splendid view far below of the old 'Castle Folly' circa 1931, with its distinctive green copper spire.

16. Your path is now following an easterly direction. It is well walked by man and sheep and is easy to follow. However, after only about 200 yards you will find that it splits into an upper and lower route. You must keep to the upper route to maintain your height on the hillside. Pause here to view the hillside ahead and the valley floor.

17. Your path gradually returns to a northerly direction to pass through the remains of the old mine workings. Note the metal gate to a major mineshaft as the path becomes a grassy track leading uphill to a derelict stone building, which housed a winding engine for the mine. Note the numerous fenced off mineshafts in this area and do remember the danger warnings you passed on your walk to this point.

Old Winding House and Mine
It is hard to believe now, but fenced off mineshafts and the remains of stone buildings reveal clues to its industrial past. Copper was mined here for many years and was transported by packhorses. The Manifold Light Railway opened in 1904 to carry agricultural materials, milk and passengers. A cheese factory followed and was successful until the demise of the railway effectively returned the area to its agricultural past. Note the village of Longnor in the distance with the distinctive hills of High Wheeldon and Parkhouse and Chrome (Dragon's Back) in the background.

18. The top of Ecton Hill is now only a short distance to your right. The area is classified as 'Right to Roam' and from here you can easily divert to the hilltop and the trig point on its crown. However, the views you have already experienced will not be bettered by gaining that extra height.

19. At a point about twenty paces above the old winding-engine house, pass through a wooden gate on your left but then turn sharp right to follow a rough vehicle track around the hill in a south-easterly direction. Hulme End, your destination, can now be seen below and to your left. Follow this track until it exits onto the narrow tarmac road leading towards Hulme End.

Old Barn Wall showing Fossils
Take time to notice the fossils of ancient sea creatures in some of the old stones forming the rear of the old barn. A truly extraordinary sight.

20. At this point there is a small stone barn on your left and a stile and fingerpost by the back of that building. Turn left here to leave the road over the stile and into a field.

21. From the barn follow a northerly direction across the field towards Hulme End. You will note from waymark signs that it is the route of the 'Staffordshire Moorlands Manifold Valley Walk' and it leads to two adjoining stone houses called East Ecton and East Side, where it rejoins the Hulme End road.

22. Turn left along the road but, after about 200 yards, note the fingerpost on your right and follow its indication to leave the road through a wooden gate. Follow a northerly direction up the field towards a stone house on the hillside. Here there is a junction of paths, one passing in front of the house and the other to its side and rear. Take the stile at the rear of the house and continue in a north easterly direction to a squeezer stile by the side of a metal gate.

23. Continue ahead to pass to the left of farm buildings and leave the field over a stile and onto the Ecton to Hulme End road. Turn right to follow the road for the short distance to its junction with the Hulme End to Alstonfield road.

24. Turn left at that junction and walk down the road to the Manifold Inn and the junction with the Leek to Hartington road. Turn left towards Leek and walk the short distance to the Manifold Visitor Centre. The small stone building by the river bridge and opposite the pub is an old toll house.

25. Depending on the time, refreshments are available at the Hulme End Stores and at the café adjoining the Manifold Visitor Centre.

Manifold Visitor Centre

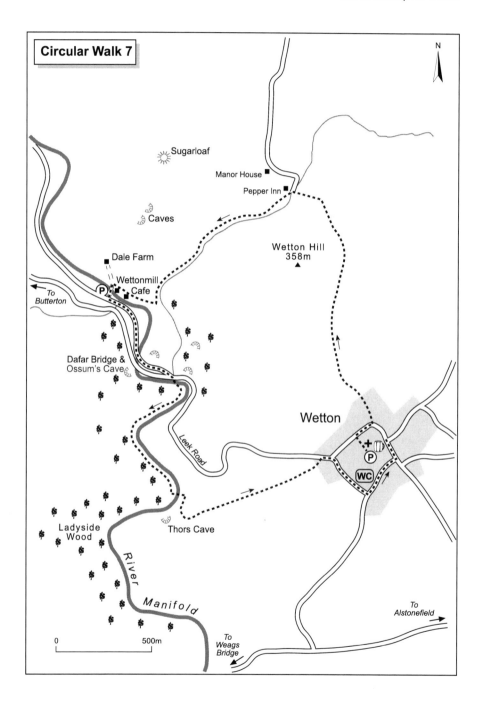

Circular Walk 7

N

Sugarloaf

Manor House

Pepper Inn

Caves

Wetton Hill
358m

Dale Farm

Wettonmill
Cafe

To
Butterton

Wetton

Dafar Bridge &
Ossum's Cave

Leek Road

Ladyside
Wood

Thors Cave

WC

River

Manifold

0   500m

To
Weags
Bridge

To
Alstonefield

Walk 7
Wetton Mill, Thor's Cave, Wetton Village, Wetton Mill

The walk starts from the rather remote location of Wetton Mill Farm and Café in the Manifold Valley. It can be accessed from the villages of Grindon, Wetton, Butterton, Warslow and Hulme End. In the first three villages expect to negotiate long and very narrow lanes, but in the last two the access roads are a little wider. For the main part, the walk provides an easy stroll through a beautiful wooded river valley followed by panoramic hilltop views and a tour around a pretty moorland village. Note however, that getting to the village and hilltops involves a rather long and steep climb. But, that effort is well rewarded by the chance to explore the ancient Thors Cave, a long past habitation of bears and mankind.

Distance	4 miles
Duration	3 hours
Parking	Wetton Mill Farm and Café (car park adjacent)
Refreshments	Wetton Mill Farm and Café, Ye Olde Royal Oak Inn, Wetton

Walk Directions

1. From the Wetton Mill Farm and Café, cross over the Manifold Valley track to enter the road, which is signed as leading to 'Butterton'. However, after only 20 yards, turn left to ford the small stream and then follow the tarmac lane towards Wetton.

2. You will soon reach the Darfar road bridge and may be surprised to see that the bed of the River Manifold is dry even though the river was seen to be in full flow at the point where you started your

Wetton Mill Café

Dafar Bridge with Ossum's Caves behind

walk. This is because at this location the waters descend through holes or 'swallets' into limestone caverns not to appear, except when the water table is high, until it reaches the area of Dovedale (see Walk 10, paragraphs 8 to 10).

3. Looking back to your start point from Dafar Bridge you will see Nan Tor Cave in the cliff above Wetton Mill. There will be an opportunity to visit that 'grotte' at the end of your walk. Looking to your right (when facing towards Wetton), you will see Ossum's Cave high above you. On the far side of the dry riverbed you may note a metal gate guarding a small entrance to the underground caverns (the area is frequented by the pot-holing fraternity).

4. Continue on the tarmac road until it reaches the location where it crosses the Manifold Track. Here, turn right to follow the track towards Waterhouses, which can often be busy with cyclists.

5. After a distance of one mile from Wetton Mill the track reaches the area of Thor's Cave, 250 feet above you and very visible on the cliff top to your left. A National Park Authority Board at the side of the

A family on holiday from Ireland view the wonders of Thor's cave

track provides interesting facts on the history of this ancient cave. Take the path to your left to cross over the river footbridge and to commence the steep climb through a dense woodland of mainly hazel trees.

6. The climb is made easy by steps provided by the National Park Authority. After several hundred yards you reach a path junction, the main route continues ahead towards Wetton and a clearly marked path on your right leads directly to the cave. Follow the path to your right and you will arrive at the 60 feet high cave entrance. A little rock climbing is necessary to enter the cave but it is well worth the effort. Looking due north, back along the route you have just followed, you will see the Nan Tor Cave above Wetton Mill (see paragraph 15 below).

7. From Thor's Cave do not return down the steps but instead follow the clearly distinct path, which circles the base of the cliff. You will circle around to your right and also upwards, until you reach a wooden gate across the path. Your eventual route to Wetton is

Seven Ways and Elderbush Caves on top of Thor's Cave

through that gate, but first turn sharp right to climb the steep path to the very top of the cliff above Thor's Cave. Take care not to get too close to the sheer cliff edges but note the magnificent views. The church you can see to the west is in the village of Grindon. Near to where you are standing you will see two small caves called Seven Ways and Elderbush. These can be explored by entering from the direction of their rear.

8. Return downhill to the wooden gate you passed on your ascent and now continue through that gate towards Wetton. Got your compass? The direction is easterly. The path is well defined but it can be muddy due to the presence of cattle.

9. At the top of the field cross over a wall by the side of a metal farm gate and onto a grassy track known as Thor's Lane. Turn left along the lane, through a further farm gate and continue to the tarmac road leading into Wetton Village.

10. You turn right along the road towards the village but, after only 20 yards or so, turn right again into the lane, which is signed to 'Grindon and Manifold Valley'. The aim now is to walk around the village and so when you reach the next road junction turn left (signed to 'Alstonfield and Dovedale') and note, just around the corner, the old village well.

11. Continue past the car park and toilets and again turn left at the next road junction to head towards the village centre where you will find the Royal Oak public house and a small

Wetton Village and Church

village green with seats. Go past the pub and the adjacent house called Royal Oak Cottage and immediately turn left to take the path into the grounds of the village church, which is well worth a visit.

12. You continue through the church grounds to reach the road by the side of the village hall (old school). Turn right here passing in front of the village hall and continue for about 150 yards to where the road bears sharply right back towards the village centre. At this point, you leave the tarmac road to turn left along the track, which passes Pig Cottage and Hill Farm Cottage. A metal signpost indicates that this track leads to 'Back of Ecton' and this, indeed, is your route.

13. Continue up the track until it terminates on reaching a closed-in water reservoir on your right. Continue straight ahead passing through a gate and then a stone squeezer stile. After only a very short distance, you reach the hilltop to pass through a further squeezer stile plus gate and enter onto the National Trust area of

Nan Tor Cave

Wetton Hill (note the metal sign). The hilltop views are superb. Note the spire of Grindon Church now on your left. From the village your compass direction has been north-westerly and it remains so until you reach the next stile where you bear slightly right – compass direction now northerly.

14. From here it is all downhill (note the hamlet of Back of Ecton directly ahead). A convenient stone wall close to your left negates the need for a compass. Follow the wall, which will turn sharply left at two locations as you walk towards the bottom of the hill. Eventually you are heading due west and directly towards a three storey stone house on the valley floor known as Pepper Inn.

House claimed to be the Pepper Inn
Whilst on this walk we met a descendant of the family who lived here. It is claimed that the dwelling used to be the 'Pepper Inn' catering for those working the Ecton copper mines in the 18th Century. Later it is said to have become an isolation hospital for contagious diseases and then a button factory.

15. Enter the lane in front of the stone house and turn left towards Wetton Mill, as indicated by the footpath finger post. You pass through a farm gate and follow a wide grass track downhill through an impressive narrow valley. After about ¼ mile you reach a point where the relatively straight path bears sharply to the left. At this location you will see a smaller path on your right. It is indicated by a footpath fingerpost as a bridleway (blue coloured sign). Take this bridleway to climb uphill in a south-easterly direction. Pass through a gate to reach the hilltop and you will then see a single post bearing a footpath direction sign. Here you turn sharply right, as indicated by that sign, and proceed downhill through trees and vegetation (compass direction now north-westerly). You will see a fence and farm gate in front of you and, just before reaching that point, the ground opens out left and right to reveal the River Manifold and Wetton Mill Farm and café below and to your left and the Nan Tor Cave directly ahead.

16. Take time to explore the cave and enjoy the southerly views along the Manifold Valley and towards Thor's Cave (see photograph on page 86), one mile distant. A gate on the south side of the Wetton Mill buildings gives access to the farm and café and the end of your walk.

Walk 8
Weag's Bridge, Beeston Tor, Throwley Hall, Castern Hall, Highfields and Bin Cliff Mines, Weag's Bridge

This walk provides not too strenuous exercise through beautiful countryside, which varies greatly from closed, but pretty, valley to open and extensive hilltop views. The area is popular with walkers and, in part, cyclists and for some of its length it shares its route with a Staffordshire Moorlands' 'Manifold Valley Circular Walk', the signs for which will be evident.

Distance	6 miles
Duration	3½ hours
Parking	Weag's Bridge in the Manifold Valley (access from the villages of Grindon,Wetton or Alstonfield)
Refreshments	Caravan on Weag's Bridge car park (hot/cold drinks and ice cream) weekends and school holidays only (closes at 4pm)

Walk Directions

The walk starts from the car park at Weag's Bridge and it follows the route of the long distance linear Manifold Trail Walk (Flash to Dovedale) until it reaches Rushley Bridge over the River Manifold near to the village of Ilam.

1. From the Weag's Bridge Car Park cross the Grindon to Wetton road in the direction of Waterhouses (compass bearing south). Do not take the walking/cycle track but instead walk along the farm track, which runs parallel between the cycle track and the river.

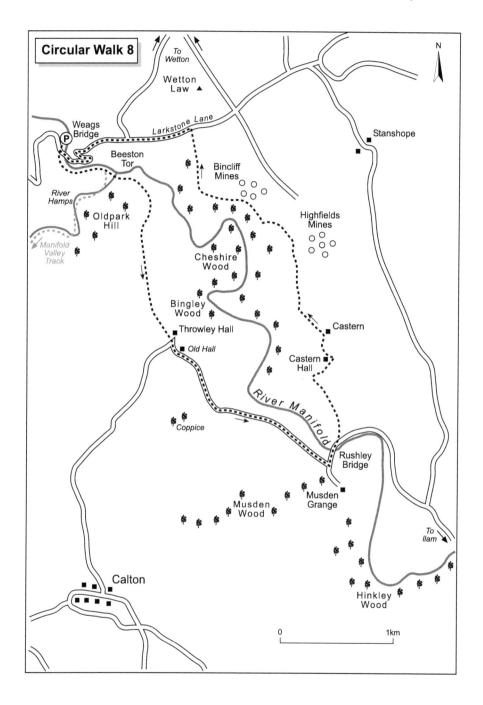

2. On reaching the site of a small caravan park, you will see an old wooden building on your right, which used to be a refreshment room catering for passengers on the railway that once ran along the valley from Waterhouses to Hulme End. At this location, you cross a river bridge, where the River Hamps joins the River Manifold.

3. After about 150 yards leave the track immediately before Beeston Tor Farm and take the path on your right, which climbs towards Throwley Hall and the village of Ilam. Now look to your left at the Beeston Tor Cliff.

4. Follow the track uphill, where the views open out as you ascend with the river and valley to the left. Pass to the right of an old stone barn and, after about 300 yards, you reach a large wooden gate blocking the track. Bear to your left, as indicated by waymark signs on the gate, leaving the track to climb up the hill on its left.

Beeston Tor Farm with Beeston Tor Cave in the limestone cliff behind. During 1924, a horde of Anglo-Saxon silver was found in the cave

5. After reaching the top of the steep hill, exit the field through a wooden gate and continue directly ahead towards Throwley Hall Farm, still out of sight but only a few hundred yards distant. On nearing the farm cross over the well defined farm track, to bear slightly right crossing the field and heading for the row of trees. Enter the farm between the buildings, entering by the gate bearing a waymark sign. Keep straight ahead through the farmyard and exit onto the tarmac road leading to Ilam. The ruins of Throwley Old Hall can be seen on the left. They are open to the public and an information board is provided and is of interest.

6. Follow the road along the valley side and pass Rushley Farm on your right. Here, the road bears sharply left to reach Rushley Bridge over the River Manifold. Immediately after the bridge, and on your left, you will see a stile, which you now need to cross into fields leading to Castern Hall. At this point you have left the Manifold Trail Walk, which continues to Ilam. Your path along the fields is very evident and well signed. Your compass bearing is now northerly.

Rushley Bridge

7. Climb uphill until the path exits onto the tarmac road leading to Castern Hall and Farm. Follow that road, passing the front of the house, and enter the area of the farm at the rear. The road bears left around the buildings and immediately on exiting, it bears right towards Castern. Just before that bend, close to the buildings and on your left, you will see a footpath finger post and a footpath on your left. A sign on the post indicates the 'Staffordshire Moorlands Manifold Valley Circular Walk' and it is that path to the left that you need to take (compass bearing now westerly).

8. Walk steadily uphill with good views on your left. The highest point you can see is Mere Hills and Tumulus. The path is well marked

Castern Hall
Home of the Hurt family since the 16th Century. The present
house was rebuilt in 1730 and there are Roman remains in the
foundations. The old house has been the location of many well
known TV dramas such as Jane Eyre, Sherlock Holmes, The Hound
of the Baskervilles, Agatha Christie's Poirot, Far from the Madding
Crowd and Jonathon Creek. The hall on occasions is made open to
the public. For details go to www.casterne.co.uk

and you pass through several stiles towards the hilltop (note
Throwley Hall Farm and the ruins of the Hall on the opposite side
of the valley).

9. At the top of the hill the path bears left to a nearby squeezer stile
   at a location known as Castern Wood Nature Reserve. Through the
   squeezer stile bear right (compass direction north-west) and keep
   the stone wall close to your right as the path circles around the
   crown of the hill. Very steeply down to your left is the Manifold

Valley with Throwley Hall and Farm on the opposite hillside. The views are superb.

10. After a short distance, you will see rough and disturbed land behind the wall on your right. This is the site of the old Highfields Mines. A little further on you cross a stile bearing an 'Access Land' sign and here you will enter the area previously occupied by the old Bin Cliff Mines. Below and to your left are Beeston Tor and Beeston Tor Farm.

11. Continue to follow the line of the wall on your right until the very distinct path drops away to the left to lead you to steps over a stone wall. Your compass direction is now north. Cross the field to a stone squeezer stile and then continue on to exit onto the tarmac Larkstone Lane. Turn left along the lane to commence a lengthy stroll downhill to the Manifold Valley and Weag's Bridge. From the bridge turn right, to enter the car park at your starting point.

Larkstone Lane

Walk 9
Ilam, Coldwall Bridge, Dovedale, Ilam

This walk is a family stroll through pleasant pastureland. It follows the course of the River Manifold to its junction with the River Dove and then continues alongside the Dove to Coldwall Bridge. The return path tracks the River Dove to Dovedale Car Park and then continues onwards to Ilam Village.

Distance	3 miles
Duration	2 hours
Parking	In Ilam Village or on the National Trust Car Park Ilam Hall (Note: Pay & Display if not a member)
Refreshments	National Trust Café in Ilam Hall or Dovedale Car Park. Toilets at Ilam Hall & Car Park Dovedale

Walk Directions

1. Start the walk at the Ilam Cross in the village centre. The impressive structure is also known as the Mary Watts Memorial. Cross over the river bridge (see photograph on page 97) on the Blore side of the Ilam Cross and leave the road by the steps and stile, which are by the left side of the bridge.

2. Follow the riverbank, which is on your left, in a southerly direction over several fields until you enter a small copse of trees. At this point the path climbs above the river, and you will need to look very closely to your left to see the River Manifold entering the River Dove as a tributary.

3. This is the place where the Manifold Trail Walk ends but this stroll now continues alongside the River Dove towards a large stone

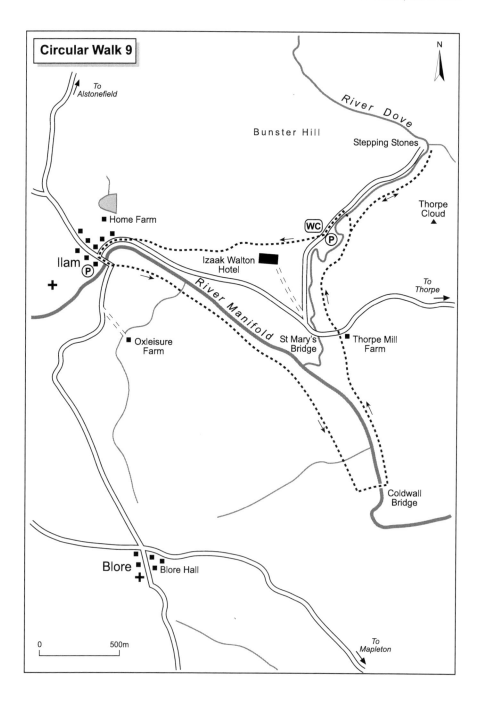

bridge known as 'Coldwall'. The path gradually leaves the riverside but the river remains in sight until the bridge eventually comes into view.

4. Your path exits the field to the right of the bridge and onto a track, which forms part of the Limestone Way Long Distance Walk. Turn left along the track to pass over the Coldwall River Bridge and, as the path begins to rise, take the stile on your left on the far side of the bridge. This returns you to the side of the river, which you will follow in a northerly direction back towards Ilam Village.

5. Just before the point where the two rivers meet, your path bears right to cross fields and exit onto the Ilam to Thorpe road. Turn left along the road but, after only 20 paces and immediately before

Ilam village river bridge
Constructed to replace St Bertram's Bridge, after the village was rebuilt away from the front of Ilam Hall, under the instructions of Jesse Watts-Russell so as not to obstruct his views

reaching the nearby road bridge, turn right along a short path and through a gate into a field. Keep to the left of the field heading towards the River Dove to reach a further gate by the riverside. Then follow the riverbank to pass the Dovedale car park, which is on the opposite side of the river. Your path exits the fields at the footbridge over the river. Cross over the bridge and turn left to reach the car park.

6. Toilets and sometimes refreshments are usually available at the car park. Leave the road as you pass the toilets in order to turn right onto the adjoining limestone track. After only about 50 paces turn right to climb steps onto a path, which passes through a small copse of trees. Leave the copse over a stile and into a field. You are walking directly towards Ilam Village in a westerly direction. Note the Isaac Walton Hotel nearby on your left and the very impressive Bunster Hill on your right.

7. Your route is straight ahead over five fields and there are numerous footpath direction signs (waymarks) to indicate your direction. You leave the final field onto the Ilam to Thorpe road. Turn right here to walk the short distance to your starting point at Ilam Cross.

Walk 10
Ilam, River Lodge via Paradise Walk, Ilam

This walk is a pleasant and informative family stroll around Ilam Village. For its greater part the walk can be suitable for the use of pushchairs but a stile followed by a multitude of steps curtails their use over the latter part of the route at the rear of Ilam Hall, which is detailed at paragraphs 6, 7 and 8.

Distance	2½ miles
Duration	Approximately 2 hours including viewing time
Parking	In Ilam village
Refreshments	National Trust café in Ilam Hall. Toilets at Ilam Hall

Walk Directions

You start the walk from the Ilam Cross in the village centre. This beautiful centre-piece to the village is also known as the Mary Watts Memorial.

1. From the Memorial Cross, walk in a northerly direction to take the Stanshope road, which passes the village school.

2. Make your way past the bus garage and onwards to the village school on your right.

   Note the lovely Swiss Alpine cottages on your right. According to information displayed at the National Trust Exhibition Room at Ilam Hall, the cottages were created in the 1820s, when Jesse Watts-Russell, the then owner of Ilam Hall, remodelled the village. It is claimed that the cottages resemble buildings seen by Watts-Russell in Switzerland.

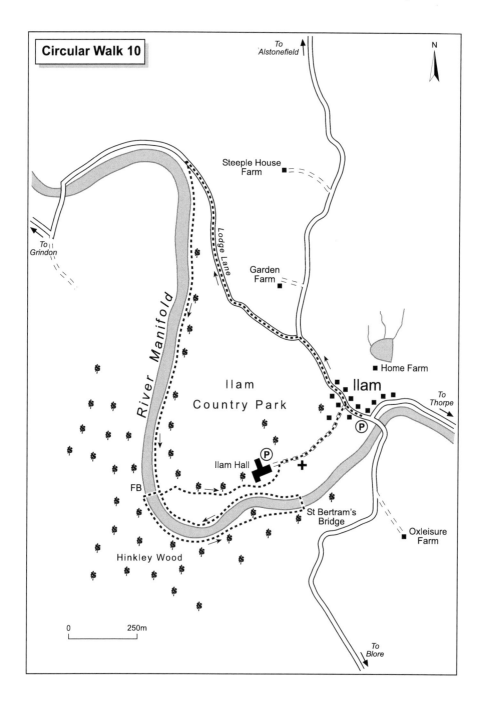

Circular Walk 10

To Alstonefield

N

Steeple House Farm

To Grindon

Lodge Lane

Garden Farm

River Manifold

Home Farm

Ilam

Ilam

To Thorpe

Ilam Country Park

P

P

Ilam Hall

FB

St Bertram's Bridge

Oxleisure Farm

Hinkley Wood

0   250m

To Blore

Illam Village School
The architecture of the school resembles that of the cottages and the building is certainly unique. In the grounds of the school near to the roadside is a small statue erected to the memory of the children lost in the Indian Ocean Tsunami of 2004

3. Climb the hill past the school and onwards to the nearby road junction. Take Lodge Lane, the road on your left, which is signed Castern and Throwley. To your left you now have a beautiful view over the typical English pastures of Ilam Hall.

4. The road eventually descends towards the River Manifold but, as you near the bottom of the hill, you will reach the pretty cottage known as River Lodge Cottage, which has a carved sign over the door stating that the last stone of River Lodge was laid on 6th May 1840 by Jemma Countess of Monteglas. The garden of the cottage is on your left and a footpath sign indicates a path which passes through the garden and onto the side of the River Manifold. Take this path through the garden and note the collection box on your left into which you may care to deposit a few coins. Why? Because the path through the garden and all the paths followed by this walk, through the grounds of Ilam Park and Hall, prior to reaching Ilam Church, are not public right of ways, but only concessionary footpaths, access to which is by kind permission of the cottage owner and the National Trust.

5. The path alongside the river is known as Paradise Walk. In summer, you are likely to find the river to be very low or even dry in places. This is due to the limestone rock structure and the fact that the river waters have descended into 'swallets' to flow underground for considerable distances (see Walk 7, paragraph 2). Follow the path alongside the river until you reach the point where a footbridge spans the river on your right. Note that the path ahead divides. To your left it climbs uphill and straight ahead, passing through a gate to follow the river. Continue straight ahead and note that a small area of grassland is now between your path and the river.

6. After about 200 yards you will reach a wooden stile in the wire fence on your right.

Note: If you have a pushchair you are recommended to leave the walk at this point and to continue straight ahead until you reach the nearby 'Battle Stone' on your left (see following paragraphs 9 and 10). There you will take the path on your left to climb uphill to the Ilam Hall Tea Rooms and the National Trust Shop.

7. Otherwise: Take the stile in the wire fence and cross the small field to the footbridge over the river. You have now reached Hinkley Wood and your path follows alongside the right of the river in an easterly direction. You climb many steps, as you pass through the wood, but the river always remains in view on your left.

8. At the point where you have descended to river level, you will see the waters passing over a small weir. In summer the river above the weir can be low and slow moving, but below the weir the river will be in full flow. The reason for this phenomenon is holes in the riverbed, known as 'boil holes'. This is the location where the waters which had disappeared underground through the 'swallets' (see paragraph 5) 'boil' to the surface to rejoin the river bed. This and other interesting information is usually available at the National Trust exhibition room adjacent to their shop at Ilam Hall. It is said that dye put into the river at Wetton Mill in the Manifold Valley took twenty four hours to emerge from the boil-holes at Ilam Hall.

9. Your path continues to St Bertram's Bridge over which you cross the river, towards Ilam Hall. National Trust literature informs that

the road bridge near to the Ilam Cross was built by Jesse Watts-Russell to avoid the road from Blore passing through Ilam Park over St Bertram's Bridge.

10. After crossing the bridge, turn sharp left to return upstream, with the river on your left. You are now heading in a westerly direction. On reaching the small weir described in paragraph 8, take time to have a close look at the site where the 'boil holes' recharge the waters of the river. Also note the waters entering the river from the small grotto on your right of the path. These are the waters of the River Hamps, which have travelled underground from the area of Waterhouses.

11. Continue along the path and, on reaching the end of a low ornate wall on your left, note the large standing 'Battle Stone' on your right side of the path.

12. At this point there is a path to the right of the Battle Stone, which climbs steeply towards Ilam Hall. Take this path and it will lead you directly to the café and tea rooms. From here, you are but a very short distance from the village centre and your starting point at Ilam Cross.

13. However, before returning to the Cross, take time to explore Ilam Hall, its grounds, the Italian Garden, the National Trust Shop and Exhibition Room. To return to the village centre you must pass the ancient church, which is usually open, dedicated to St Bertram, containing the Watts-Russell Memorial.

This is known as the 'Battle Stone' dated to the 11th Century and associated with the struggle between the Saxons and the Danes

Did you know that what you see at Ilam Hall is in fact little more than the servant's quarters and stable block? A visit to the Trust's Exhibition Room can reveal its interesting history, its magnificence during the 19th century, its use as a luxury hotel in the 1920s, its partial demolition during the 1930s and its present successful use by the National Youth Hostel Association.

above: *View of Ilam Church, Bunster Hill and Thorpe Cloud from the Manifold Tea Rooms*

right: *Watts Memmorial inside Illam Church*

Walk 11
Ilam Village, Dovedale, Ilam Rock, Dovedale Wood, Ilam Tops, Bunster Hill, Ilam Village

This walk commences with a stroll along the beautiful and popular Dovedale Valley with its interesting geographical features and ends with a walk along the high ridges of Bunster Hill, from where the views rival any to be found in England. In between, there is a steep but pretty climb through Dovedale Wood, which may well test the lungs.

Distance	5 miles
Duration	3½ hours
Parking	On road at Ilam Village Centre or the National Trust Car Park Ilam Hall (Note: Pay & Display if not a member)
Refreshments	National Trust Café in Ilam Hall; Caravan at Dovedale car park during weekends and school holidays. Toilets at Ilam Hall and Dovedale car park

Walk Directions

1. Commence the walk from the centre of Ilam by the Mary Watts Memorial Cross. Take the Thorpe road, which follows the left and Staffordshire side of the River Manifold towards Dovedale.

2. After a little less than 200 yards you pass the pretty Town End Cottage on your left, and at the end of the cottage garden you need to leave the road through a gate on your left, which bears a sign 'Access Land' (Right to Roam). Behind the gate a metal sign

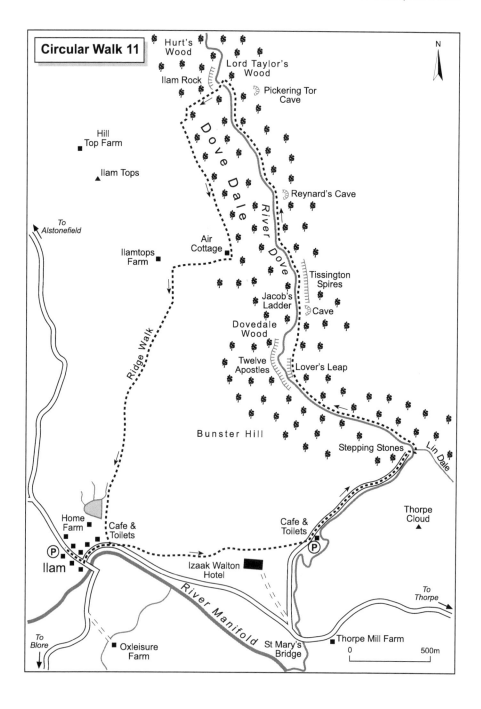

Circular Walk 11

Hurt's Wood
Lord Taylor's Wood
Ilam Rock
Pickering Tor Cave
N
Dove Dale
Hill Top Farm
Ilam Tops
Reynard's Cave
River Dove
To Alstonefield
Air Cottage
Ilamtops Farm
Tissington Spires
Jacob's Ladder
Cave
Dovedale Wood
Ridge Walk
Twelve Apostles
Lover's Leap
Bunster Hill
Stepping Stones
Lin Dale
Home Farm
Cafe & Toilets
Cafe & Toilets
Thorpe Cloud
P
Ilam
Izaak Walton Hotel
P
To Thorpe
River Manifold
To Blore
Oxleisure Farm
St Mary's Bridge
Thorpe Mill Farm
0   500m

Town End Cottage

announces your entry onto National Trust land at Bunster Hill. Look high above to your left to see the hilltops, which you will descend to terminate your walk.

3. Turn right through the gate and follow the clearly marked path in an easterly direction, over several fields, towards Dovedale. Pass close by the Isaac Walton Hotel on your right to arrive at the Dovedale car park. Toilets are available and a mobile refreshment caravan provides food and drinks at weekends and during school holidays.

4. From the car park turn left to walk upstream in a northerly direction and, on reaching the river footbridge, note the National Trust Information Board with its interesting facts. Here you have a decision to make. You need to cross the River Dove to reach its right side and the County of Derbyshire. Most people make the easy crossing over the bridge to walk upstream beneath Thorpe Cloud Hill; but note that the ground is rough underfoot. Alternatively, you can continue in comfort on the Staffordshire side of the river until

you reach the stepping-stones, which provide a crossing; certainly a more adventurous route but perhaps a little precarious. Note however that the stepping stones may be under water when the river is high. The stepping stones crossing has been in place since the late 19th century and, during the 1950s, it was an area of mass tourism with stalls and even donkey rides.

5. Your walk takes you along the excellent path on the Derbyshire side of the river. The scenery is superb, at least equal to that of the Suffolk 'Constable' countryside. It is now hard to visualise but, during Victorian times, there were few trees and vegetation on the valley sides, and the high and jagged cliffs were easy to view.

6. The first cliffs you are now likely to see through the dense woodland on your left are known as Dovedale Castle.They are immediately on the left at the point where your previously flat footpath rises steeply upwards before falling quickly back to river level.

The Stepping Stones at Dovedale

Reynard's Cave
Named after a local robber who took refuge in the cave. The arch was formed after the roof fell in. Artefacts from the Bronze Age found in the cave are on display in Buxton Museum. Several tales have been told about the cave. One being that, until her death in 1899, a woman from Mill Dale placed a rope up to the archway every day in hope of a monetary tip. Another, that an Irish dean was out riding with a young girl. The horse slipped and all three fell down the slope. He died from his injuries and is buried at Ashbourne.

7. After a short distance the path again rises, this time assisted by steps and on your left you may see the cliffs, known as 'Twelve Apostles', through the trees. The steps take you to a high point above the river known as Lover's Leap (it is claimed that some lovelorn person once did so but fortunately survived to lead the life of a spinster).

Lion Head Rock

8. The next rock formation on your right are vertical cliffs known as Tissington Spires. You may see rock climbers. Continue on to where the remains of an old brick pump house are on the right of the path and look over the river on your left to see the cliff known as Dovedale Church.

9. Next on your right is a natural stone archway known as Reynard's Cave (see photograph on previous page).

10. After traversing the wooden walkway by the riverside a high cliff closely borders the path. Can you make out the head of a lion? It is called Lion Head Rock.

11. About 200 yards further on you will see the large footbridge over which you need to cross the river. The tall cliff on the Staffordshire side of the river is Ilam Rock, a favourite challenge for rock climbers. On the Derbyshire side, the cliffs are known as Pickering Tor. Cross the bridge, but pause halfway to look back through the

trees to the furthest of the Pickering Tor cliffs. At times when leaves have fallen, you can see a cube of rock seemingly balanced on the cliff top. This is the 'Watchbox' and it is said that, in Victorian Times, "it could be made to rock on its precarious perch". Much of this area is cared for by the National Trust.

12. Cross the bridge and follow the river upstream for some 300 yards to a location where you will find a junction of footpaths and a National Trust direction sign. Here you turn left to climb steeply uphill and through the dense Dovedale Wood.

13. The path zig-zags upwards and you are assisted by steps on the steep hillside. When you reach the top of the woodland, follow the path around to your left. The path is very clear and takes a southerly direction towards Ilam along the hilltop and parallel to the valley floor.

Bridge by Illam Rock

14. At the end of the woodland, the path exits through a gate onto farmland. Immediately ahead you will see Air Cottage and to your right is a distinct grass track leading to those buildings. However, note the direction indicated by the footpath fingerpost, which takes you slightly left and lower down the hill to enter trees, where you will find a reassuring footpath sign.

15. Follow the path clearly marked below and to the left of Air Cottage, bearing right around the cottage to exit onto the cottage driveway/track. Turn left and you will reach Ilam Tops Farm where

Best possible view of Ilam

you are confronted by a stone wall and farm gate. Do not pass through the gate but turn sharp left to follow a line of trees in a southerly direction towards Bunster Hill.

16. After the trees, you pass a stone barn on your left and then continue on to follow the line of the stone wall on your right. You will arrive at a gate where a National Trust sign announces that you are approaching Bunster Hill (Access Land – Right to Roam).

17. Through the gate there are footpaths to the right and to the left, but taking advantage of the right to roam you continue straight ahead, climbing steeply uphill to follow the high ridges of Bunster Hill. Your route is southerly, with the Manifold Valley far below on your right. Continue to wander over the highest points until the hillside falls away on your left to reveal Dovedale, its car park and the Thorpe road.

18. Continue until you reach the point where you must commence to descend. From this most magnificent viewpoint you can see the River Dove and the River Manifold. Look slightly southeast (left) and you will see where the two rivers join. On your right note Ilam Hall and its grounds, the rear of the village school and cottages.

19. Directly ahead and below there is a very distinctive and narrow final ridge leading towards the Thorpe road, which is well within view. Your route is directly across that ridge at the end of which you have the best possible view of the lovely Staffordshire village of Ilam.

20. Descend steeply down from the ridge and make for the gate onto the Thorpe road, which is alongside the garden of Town End Cottage. Turn right to pass by the cottage to reach the village centre.

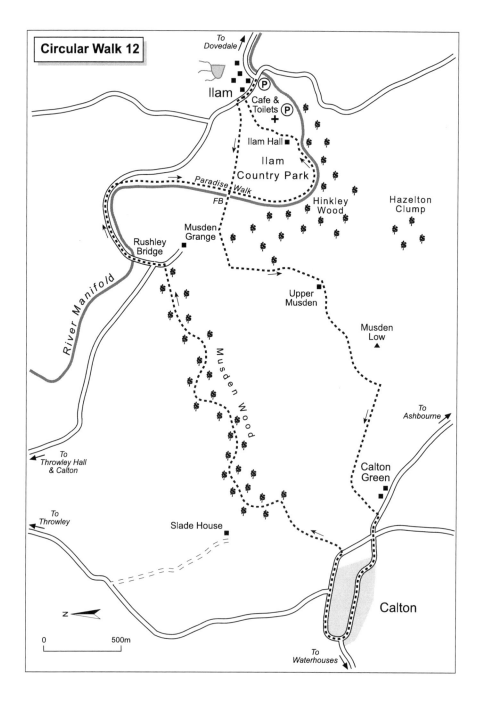

Circular Walk 12

Walk 12
Ilam, Calton, Musden Grange, Ilam

Although of short mileage, this walk requires warm and waterproof clothing for high places, stout boots for wet and muddy sections and lungs in good order for a steep climb. That said, the effort and minor discomforts endured are well rewarded by interesting and varied scenery and impressive high views.

Distance	6½ miles
Duration	4 hours
Parking	In Ilam Village or on the National Trust car park at Ilam Hall (Note: Pay & Display if not a member)
Refreshments	National Trust Café at Ilam Hall. Toilets at Ilam Hall

Walk Directions

1. The walk commences from Ilam village centre where stands the Ilam Cross and the pretty village cottages. Pass by the cottages to follow the Stanshope road to the village school, just a short distance from the entrance driveway to Ilam Hall.

2. Directly opposite the school gates note the footpath fingerpost and take the stile which is on your left. You are now in the grounds of Ilam Park with its sheep cropped grass and imposing mature trees. The path follows an old limestone track, which is indistinct due to increasing grass cover.

3. Your compass direction is due west and, after about 400 yards, note that your footpath leaves the track to the right, keeping to the

bearing of due west (helpful waymark signs confirm your route at this point).

4. After a short distance, the path descends steeply to a pathway, which runs parallel to the River Manifold. Cross over this path to reach a footbridge over the river and pass over to a small field. From there you follow a north westerly direction to a stone squeezer stile at the base of a hill.

5. At this point waymark signs indicate a popular path to your right and another which continues straight ahead. You continue ahead and proceed uphill in a westerly direction. This path is very indistinct but, after only a short distance, a gap can be seen in the stone wall at the top of the field.

6. Pass through the wall and your compass bearing is now south-westerly. From here you face a rather steep climb, but look behind as you stop for breath to appreciate the impressive view towards

Illam Cross

Bunster Hill and Thorpe Cloud. The ascent is short but several hundred feet are climbed over the relatively short distance of about ¼ mile.

7. On nearing the top of the field, you will see a stone wall directly ahead. Bear left at this point to take a southerly direction to the top left corner of the field. Cross the ladder stile and continue due south towards Hazleton Clump, a hill which is directly ahead of you with its very distinct top-not of trees.

8. The path climbs gradually uphill and you will follow the line of a stone wall on your right. At the top of that hill, and well before Hazleton Clump, you will see a wooden stile in the wall on your right. Pass over that stile and cross the field to the left corner of a derelict stone barn. Climb the wall by the side of the barn to reach the footpath fingerpost and ladder stile, just a few paces to your left. That fingerpost indicates your southerly path to the village of Calton. Cross the ladder stile and a further one just 20 yards distant.

9. Pass to the left of the derelict farmhouse and, at the end of the hedgerow, which marks the boundary of the property, bear right to a fingerpost that indicates a junction of paths. Bear left here, to follow the line of a stone wall on your left. Exit the field through a stone squeezer stile and bear right to head due west around the hill ahead. Cross diagonally to your right, up and around the hill until a stone wall appears directly ahead. At this point veer slightly left to the south-west and you will arrive at a stile in the wall.

10. Continue south-west to a stile in a stone wall. Turn sharp right as indicated by the waymark sign and follow the line of the wall on your right until you leave the field by way of a stile onto a farm driveway. Turn right along the driveway and, after only a short distance, you enter a farmyard with gates and buildings blocking the way ahead. Your footpath is on the left of the yard, directly opposite the farmhouse and somewhat hidden by vegetation. Pass through that stile to enter a field and continue ahead, still in a south-westerly direction. Cross a stone wall and follow the indication of the waymark sign, keeping to the line of the stone

wall on your right. After only about 100 paces, you will see a stile in the wall on your right. Cross into the next small field and walk diagonally left to exit onto a tarmac road, leading to the village of Calton.

11. Turn right along that road and, after about 150 yards, you reach a crossroads. Continue straight ahead (signed 'Calton and Waterhouses') and walk through the village passing the small, ancient church on your right (usually open) and the village hall on your left.

12. Continue through the village and you will reach a junction with a metal direction sign. At this point turn right towards Ilam and Throwley, passing Town End Farm and Town End House.

13. On reaching the next road junction, which has a direction sign indicating a left turn to Ilam and Throwley, continue straight ahead

A chance of a rest at the crossroads

Looking back to Thorpe Cloud and Bunster Hill

and downhill until the road bears sharply to the right. Here there is a small sewage pumping station on your left and, just 30 paces further on, you will see a fingerpost indicating a footpath on your left.

14. Leave the road by a gate at that point and continue ahead keeping the boundary hedge on your right. Pass through a further gate and commence a gradual descent through Musden Wood. Your compass direction is north-east and the path is distinct and easy to follow. Note however that during periods of damp weather the path can be wet underfoot and extremely muddy. The path through the wood is also long (about 1½ miles) but very pretty.

15. Exit the woods at Musden Grange onto a tarmac track, near to farm buildings. Turn left to pass by the buildings and join the Manifold Trail Walk just before the Rushley Bridge over the River Manifold. From this point you can easily follow the distinctive Manifold Trail waymark signs, which lead to Ilam Village Centre, but first follow the road over the river bridge.

16. As the road begins to rise, River Lodge Cottage (1840) is on the right. Leave the road and take the concessionary path to the right through the garden of the cottage and onto National Trust land to walk alongside the left of the river.

Note that all paths through the grounds of Ilam Hall on the route of this walk are not public rights of way until you have passed by the Ilam Church. They are, in fact, concessionary paths; public use being permitted by kind permission of the National Trust.

17. Follow the river into the grounds of Ilam Hall keeping the river within sight. On the left by the side of the path, note the 'Battle Stone' dated to the 11th Century and associated with the struggle between the Saxons and the Danes.

Ilam Hall was once a large and magnificent Victorian Gothic manor house, but during the 1930s the main hall and formal rooms were demolished leaving only that part which mainly housed the servants quarters. However, the remaining building is still very impressive and now houses a Youth Hostel providing over 100 beds with family rooms available. It is an excellent base for walkers and is very popular with families, groups and large parties.

18. Before leaving the grounds, note that the National Trust Café and Tea Rooms situated behind the Hall offer substantial refreshments. The adjoining Trust Shop has attractive and varied products and there are often interesting displays in the Exhibition Centre next door.

19. Exit the grounds by passing alongside the left side of the ancient church to turn left along the pathway, which leads to the village centre.

Acknowledgements

Our thanks to Phil and Chris Poole, Mel and Chris Griffiths, Colin and Ann Sherwin, Greg and Jean Jackson and George and Audrey James, in appreciation of the 'proof-walking' of the 12 circular walks without the aid of an Ordnance Survey map and their valued advice which followed. Also to the Ramblers' Association Stoke/Newcastle-under-Lyme Group for their help and assistance in the production of this guide.

Thanks also to Paul Mortimer, Projects Office, National Trust, Ilam in appreciation of his co-operation and valued advice.

Appreciation is shown for the considerable help and co-operation afforded by the Staffordshire County Council Countryside Directorate without whose assistance the recording of this walking guide would not have been possible.

Also from Sigma Leisure:

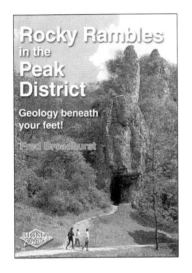

Rocky Rambles in The Peak District
Fred Broadhurst

"The Peak District has a dramatic story to tell and Fred Broadhurst is just the guide we need." – Aubrey Manning, presenter of the BBC TV series 'Earth Story'.

You don't have to be an expert or even an amateur geologist to enjoy these 'rocky rambles'! Where better than in and around the Peak District would you find geology right there beneath your feet - all you need to know is where to look.

The comprehensive glossary of terms, which covers the identification of Peak District Rocks, forms an invaluable supplement and provides 'at a glance' information for the reader.

£8.99

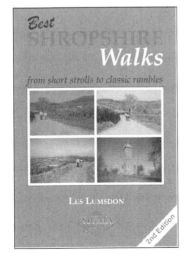

Best Shropshire Walks 2nd Edition
From short strolls to classic rambles
Les Lumsdon

A new revised edition of this much loved guide contains 36 walks, including 12 completely new routes, located in all parts of the county. Several walks feature fine hill walking on the Welsh borders and others start from delightful villages and hamlets in the north and east of the county.

£8.99

Archaeology Walks in the Peak District
Ali Cooper

Put on your walking boots, enjoy the superb scenery of the Peak District and enjoy a roller-coaster ride through history with Ali Cooper. Routes ranging from 3 to 12 miles explore Peak District sites where there are visible features in the landscape. Brief descriptions of the major finds on the walks are included, plus a bibliography for those who want to delve deeper.

"... a new authoritative book ... for a spot of time travel while out walking" – Derby Evening Telegraph

£8.99

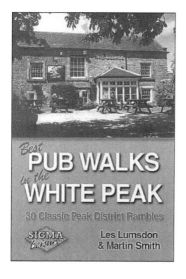

Best Pub Walks in the White Peak
30 Classic Peak District Rambles
Les Lumsden & Martin Smith

The 30 fabulous walks range from three to nine miles and ideal for family rambles. They start in such delightful Peak District villages as Ashford-in-the-Water, Alstonefield and Youlgreave, most of which are accessible by public transport — so that you can leave the car at home and savour the products on offer at the authors' favourite pubs.

Follow the recommendatios in this well-established — and completely updated — book for a superb variety of walks in splendid scenery and, after each walk, relax in a Peak District pub renowned for its welcome to walkers and for the quality of its Real Ale, often supplied by local independent brewers.

£7.95

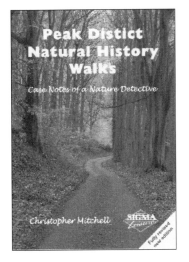

Peak District Walking Natural History Walks
Christopher Mitchell

An updated 2nd Edition with 18 varied walks for all lovers of the great outdoors — and armchair ramblers too! Learn how to be a nature detective, a 'case notes' approach shows you what clues to look for and how to solve them. Detailed maps include animal tracks and signs, landscape features and everything you need for the perfect natural history walk. There are mysteries and puzzles to solve to add more fun for family walks — solutions supplied! Includes follow on material with an extensive Bibliography and 'Taking it Further' sections.

£8.99

Best Tea Shop Walks in the Peak District
Norman and June Buckley

A wonderful collection of easy-going walks that are ideal for families and all those who appreciate fine scenery with a touch of decandence in the shape of an afternoon tea or morning coffee —or both! The 26 walks are spread widely across the Peak District, including Lyme Park, Castleton, Miller's Dale, and The Roaches and — of course — such famous dales as Lathkill and Dovedale. Each walk has a handy summary so that you can choose the walks that are ideally suited to the interests and abilities of your party. The tea shops are just as diverse, ranging from the splendour of Chatsworth House to more basic locations. Each one welcomes ramblers and there is always a good choice of tempting goodies.

£7.95

Derbyshire Walks with Children
William D Parke

There are 24 circular walks, ranging from 1 to 6 miles in length, and each one has been researched and written with children in mind. The directions and background information have been checked and revised as necessary for this updated reprint.

Detailed instructions for parents and an interactive commentary for children mean there's never a dull moment. There are even 'escape routes' to allow families to tailor each walk to suit their own needs, time and energy.

"The needs, entertainment and safety of children have been of paramount importance."
– Peak Advertiser
£8.99

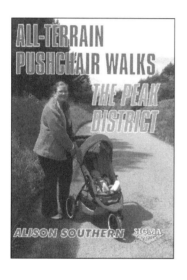

All-Terrain Pushchair Walks:
The Peak District
Alison Southern

The Peak District, in the heart of the country, has some of England's most picturesque landscapes, from the White Peak in the south with its rocky outcrops and steep hills, to the Dark Peak in the north with peat moss moorland and stunning vistas. This book is for families with all-terrain pushchairs and buggies, and for everyone wishing to avoid as many stiles and obstacles as possible. Includes family-friendly attractions, trees to identify, birds and plants to spot, and lots more to discover. Have fun while you walk enjoying the amazing views, have some healthy exercise and spend time with the family away from the modern world.
£7.95.

Peak District Trigpointing Walks
Hill walking with a point to it!
Keith Stevens & Peter Whittaker

A superb introduction to an intriguing new walking experience: searching out all those elusive Ordnance Survey pillars. Packed with detailed walks to new and interesting Peak District summits, with a wealth of fascinating information on the history of the OS and the art of GPS navigation.

There are 150 Peak District Ordnance Survey pillars — can you find them all? Walk to all the best scenic viewpoints — from the top you can spot all the surrounding pillars. This book shows you how.
£8.95

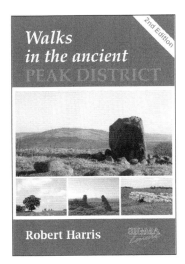

Walks in the Ancient Peak District
Robert Harris

A collection of walks visiting the prehistoric monuments and sites of the Peak District. A refreshing insight into the thinking behind the monuments, the rituals and strange behaviour of our ancestors. All the routes are circular, most starting and finishing in a town or village that is easy to locate and convenient to reach by car.
£8.99

All of our books are all available through booksellers. For a free catalogue, please contact:

SIGMA LEISURE, STOBART HOUSE, PONTYCLERC, PENYBANC ROAD AMMANFORD, CARMARTHENSHIRE SA18 3HP
Tel: 01269 593100 Fax: 01269 596116

info@sigmapress.co.uk   www.sigmapress.co.uk